Overcoming Childhood Misfortune

Overcoming Childhood Misfortune

CHILDREN WHO BEAT THE ODDS

Warren A. Rhodes
and
Kim Hoey

PRAEGER

Westport, Connecticut
London

Library of Congress Cataloging-in-Publication Data

Rhodes, Warren Allen.
    Overcoming childhood misfortune : children who beat the odds /
Warren A. Rhodes and Kim Hoey.
      p.   cm.
    Includes bibliographical references and index.
    ISBN 0-275-94081-0 (alk. paper)
    1. Children—United States—Case studies. 2. Success—United
States—Case studies. 3. Children—Conduct of life—Case studies.
I. Hoey, Kim. II. Title.
HQ792.U5R48   1994
305.23'0973—dc20   93-19611

British Library Cataloguing in Publication Data is available.

Library of Congress Catalog Card Number: 93-19611
ISBN: 0-275-94081-0

First published in 1994

Praeger Publishers, 88 Post Road West, Westport, CT 06881
An imprint of Greenwood Publishing Group, Inc.

Printed in the United States of America

The paper used in this book complies with the
Permanent Paper Standard issued by the National
Information Standards Organization (Z39.48-1984).

10 9 8 7 6 5 4 3 2 1

Contents

Acknowledgments

We greatly appreciate the willingness of our participants to share their lives with our readers. In our mutual search for answers to questions in their lives, we have brought our readers and researchers alike one step closer to understanding the roots of resiliency. This volume exists only because our participants were willing to share their lives—a task that is difficult for most and serves as a testimony to their strength.

We offer a very special thanks to Ms. Linda Haskins, assistant professor, Delaware State University for her insights, dedication, and comprehensive editorial assistance.

And to Barbara, thanks for supporting, assisting, caring, listening, loving.

Introduction

Nothing intrigues us more than a success story: whether it's rags
to riches, physical survival against overwhelmingly destructive
forces, or the victory of faith in defiance of reason—we love to
revel in the triumph of the human spirit. We find it particularly
inspiring to hear of individuals who experience devastating, potentially debilitating, emotional trauma in childhood, yet
triumph to become extraordinary, productive adults.

As a psychologist, I am often asked to explain unusual human
behavior, and by definition those who succeed despite tremendous odds against success indeed exhibit unusual, meritorious
behavior. As lead author, self-proclaimed "kindred spirit," and
one who has "succeeded despite the odds," I must admit that
my interest in understanding how individuals turn the negative
into positive was first stimulated by my own self-study. In fact,
I entered the field of psychology some twenty years ago for the
very purpose of explaining why and how such turnarounds
occur. Unfortunately, psychology has only recently begun to
systematically study the unusually good outcome. Hence, my
search for the "answers" still awaits the support of scientific
fact. This volume lives as evidence of a continued search for
those "answers."

By and large, psychology has concentrated on factors that

contribute to individuals becoming unhealthy and has paid very little attention to those individuals who become healthy when all indications would predict the opposite. To some extent, we can understand this orientation because, historically, psychology has concentrated on identifying and treating people with psychological disorders. There appeared to be no real need or motivation to explore and hence explain factors contributing to the development of the healthy personality. Admittedly, this is an oversimplification, but to provide a detailed objective evaluation of the history of psychology goes far beyond the scope of this book. Suffice it to say, therefore, that there is a wealth of information in the scientific literature that addresses why things go wrong in a person's life, but very little that seeks to explain why things go right, and even less on why things go right when they "should" go wrong. Lois Murphy (1962) explains this point very well:

In applying clinical ways of thinking formulated out of experience with broken adults, we were slow to see how the language of adequacy to meet life's challenges could become the subject matter of psychological science. Thus there are thousands of studies of maladjustment for each one that deals directly with the ways of managing life's problems with personal strength and adequacy. The language of problems, difficulties, inadequacies, of antisocial or delinquent conduct, or of ambivalence and anxiety is familiar. We know that there are devices for correcting, bypassing, or overcoming threats, but for the most part these have not been studied. (Murphy, 1962, p. 186)

This book is dedicated to the spirit expressed in Murphy's remarks. In an earlier and more technical volume on this subject (Rhodes and Brown, 1991), I spearheaded an exploration into the scientific explanation of why some children succeed despite the odds. The current volume is written for those who wish to explore the "why" of succeeding despite the odds, but do not wish to plow through a mountain of scientific literature. The current volume is an extensive investigation using a case study method of seven individuals who demonstrated extraordinary life success, despite having experienced a childhood life circumstance that would have emotionally and/or socially crippled most individuals. Our goal is to explore the factors that helped these individuals overcome the odds. In so doing, we hope that we'll shed some light on a subject that intrigues most of us but, for the most part, remains in the shadows of our psychological storehouse of knowledge.

Our sincere thanks go to those brave and trusting individuals who allowed us to intrude on their personal lives for the purpose of this investigation. Talking about their experiences awakened feelings, good and bad, that many thought were lost and forgotten. While the process, in several instances, was painful for the individuals involved, they expressed no regrets. We salute their courage.

Each chapter is divided into three major parts. The first part consists of a brief description of a difficult childhood life circumstance and the life problems that characteristically result from such a childhood experience. The second part presents the results of an extensive interview with an individual who experienced this particular childhood life circumstance but somehow "beat the odds" against healthy adjustment. The final part of the chapter highlights factors that appeared significant in helping the subject succeed when all indications were to the contrary. This part includes personality descriptions of the individual, based on interview data and results of the Sixteen Personality Factors Inventory (Cattell, Eber, and Tatsuoka 1970).

Two major assumptions underlie our investigation. First, we believe that, just as there are systematic factors leading to development of negative behaviors, so there are systematic factors leading to the development of positive behaviors. One may not always be aware of these latter factors or study them in any systematic way, but they are definitive and causative. That is, these factors contribute significantly and systematically to the individual's success. Individuals beat the odds because some combination of individual and environmental factors works to produce the extraordinary outcome; it's not just luck.

Second, the reports of individual participants are accurate representations of events that occurred. Furthermore, individuals can understand and accurately report on events, circumstances, and factors that were important in their overcoming the odds. This information can be used to formulate hypotheses and, eventually, theories to explain the development of such behaviors.

In sum, we contend that our case study method of inquiry is a valid means of obtaining information and can contribute significantly to our understanding behavior today.

Who are these individuals who succeed despite the odds? What are the significant factors contributing to their success? Basically, these two questions underlie our current inquiry. We believe the answers to these questions, if obtainable, require a combination of methods of collecting information. Initially, we were motivated to understand and possibly explain how and why some individuals succeed when others do not. Only after deciding to investigate this stimulating question did we reason that it was equally, if not more, beneficial to describe who these individuals were.

Seven individuals were ultimately chosen as the targets of our investigation. We first contacted all but three of them when they responded to a newspaper article that asked for volunteers who had succeeded despite the odds. The article appeared in a newspaper with statewide circulation. Twenty-one individuals responded to the article, and one of the investigators contacted them by telephone to determine whether their life circumstances qualified them as "succeeding despite the odds." Eight of them were excluded from the sample following repeated unsuccessful attempts to reach them. Eight others either were judged not to qualify as "succeeding despite the odds" or were excluded because investigators had already interviewed someone else who had overcome a similar life circumstance. One respondent was actually interested only in interviewing the lead investigator. The remaining four individuals were chosen as the targets of our investigation because each had indeed overcome a difficult life circumstance that, we believed, qualified them as "succeeding despite the odds." Two additional individuals not reached by the newspaper article were chosen to participate because the investigators personally knew that they qualified as subjects and had particular life circumstances that had not already been covered by the other participants. The lead investigator also served as a participant. Hence, the current investigation involves extensive study of seven individuals. The major demographic characteristics of these subjects are as follows: three females, four males, four African Americans and three Caucasians. The average age at the time of the interview was 42 years.

An intensive, open-ended interview approach was used to collect the data to answer the question, "What are the significant factors contributing to our participant's success?" Admittedly, this approach was quite subjective and, perhaps, of limited scientific value. However, we chose this approach because it provided maximum flexibility for both the participants and the investigators: we wanted the participants to feel free to openly explore and express their understanding of factors contributing to their overcoming seemingly insurmountable odds. We also wanted the freedom to gather information that simply could not be obtained in more restricted procedures, such as standardized questionnaires and closed-end interviews. Consequently, every interview took on unique characteristics: the length of the interview, the nature of the questions asked, the extent of probing, and so on, varied. All but two of the participants were interviewed solely by the second investigator. Two participants were interviewed jointly by both investigators.

While we felt that the open-ended interview gave us the best opportunity to explore each participant's understanding of factors contributing to his or her success, we felt that a more objective procedure was required to explore individual personality factors and answer the question, "Who are these individuals who succeed despite the odds?" The Sixteen Personality Factor Questionnaire (16PF) was the measure used to address this latter question. The 16PF is an extensively researched questionnaire used by psychologists, counselors, and mental health professionals to answer a variety of questions relative to personality assessment, diagnosis, career counseling, and treatment planning.

Since it was first presented to the psychological community in 1940, the 16PF has matured into one of the most important personality assessment instruments available to behavioral science professionals. Its current prominence is due, in part, to careful theoretical planning that guided its development and preceded its publication, a dedicated and active maintenance program that has kept its content and norm current during more than 39 years of dramatic cultural change, and a large and ever-expanding information data base available in approximately two thousand research publications. (Krug, 1981, p. 1)

Unlike questionnaires designed for assessment of abnormal personality, the 16PF is a test of normal personality functioning, though its use also has implications for assessment of abnormalities and therapeutic intervention. As its name implies, the 16PF measures sixteen bipolar, primary personality traits. Through extensive research, however, a number of secondary personality factors have been identified. That is, according to some experts, a combination of scores on the primary factors can yield more discriminating descriptions of personality structure. Although there are several versions of the questionnaire, the one used for this project (Form A) consists of 187 questions, written at average high school reading level, and it requires about 45 minutes for completion. The tests were scored by computer.

There are numerous ways, some rather controversial, of describing a person's personality using his or her 16PF scores. The analysis used in this investigation describes the individual's personality by focusing on the primary personality traits on which the participant had the most extreme (high or low) scores. Such analysis should, at a minimum, provide a general picture of personality traits that currently characterize the individual, and provide an opportunity to compare these characteristics to those of other participants. The 16PF is used to gauge the individual's responses today—and not necessarily to determine how they would have responded some time in the distant past. The individual's personality is a dynamic combination of biological factors and past and current life experiences. While we may be able to speculate about the participants' formative personality characteristics based on current 16PF scores, we cannot be sure that current personality characteristics contributed significantly in the individual's "succeeding despite the odds." The 16PF is used primarily to provide a description of who the individual is now and not necessarily who he was several years ago. Personality characteristics measured by the 16PF are described in the following charts.

FACTOR A

Low Scores Cool, Reserved, Detached, Aloof	**High Scores** Warm, Outgoing, Easygoing	
Individuals who scored low on this scale tend to be aloof, indifferent, and distant. They prefer things rather than people and are rigid in their thinking and behavior.	Individuals who score high, on the other hand, are easygoing, easy to warm up to, like people more than things, and can share their feelings more readily than those who score low.	

FACTOR B

Low Scores Concrete-Thinking	**High Scores** Abstract Thinking	
Low scorers on this scale tend to think concretely, are slow learners, appear dull, and usually perform poorly in school.	High scorers tend to think abstractly, find learning easier, have a quick grasp of knowledge and ideas, and tend to perform better in school.	

FACTOR C

Low Scores Easily upset, Emotionally unstable	**High Scores** Calm, Emotionally unstable	
Those who score low on FACTOR C typically are easily upset and annoyed, have low frustration tolerance, and are quite emotional.	Those scoring high are more emotionally mature, and have the necessary resources to handle life's ups and downs.	

FACTOR E

Low Scores Nonassertive, Submissive	**High Scores** Dominant, Assertive	
Individuals scoring low on this scale tend to be followers, easily led by others' points of view humble, and rather submissive.	High scorers are self-assured, strong-willed, tough-minded, more self-assertive, and forthright in expressing their views.	

FACTOR F

Low Scores
Sober

Low scorers on FACTOR F tend to be restrained, introspective, pessimistic, and very cautious.

High Scores
Enthusiastic

High scorers are usually spontaneous, careful, cheerful, and expressive.

FACTOR G

Low Scores
Expedient, Nonconforming

Individuals scoring low on FACTOR G are generally less conforming to group rules and less respectful of authority and tend to be freewheeling.

High Scores
Conforming, Conscientious

High scorers, on the other hand, are respectful of authority, follow group norms often to the letter and are real team players.

The tendency to follow group norms is not restricted to socially appropriate norms but rather to the norms of the group with which they identify.

FACTOR H

Low Scores
Shy, Timid

Individuals who score low on this scale are shy, hesitant, and sometimes consumed by feelings of inferiority.

High Scores
Bold, Venturesome

High scorers are able to endure stress with little sign of fatigue; they are bold, energetic, adventuresome, and enjoy being the center of attention.

FACTOR I

Low Scores
Tough-minded

Individuals scoring low on FACTOR I are described as realistic, tough-minded, and straight-thinking, with both feet on the ground.

High Scores
Sensitive

High scorers are day-dreamers, dependent, overprotected, insecure, temperamental, and unrealistic.

FACTOR L

Low Scores Trusting, Accepting	**High Scores** Suspicious, Distrustful
Low scorers on FACTOR L are more likely to be accepting of others, not overly jealous, and willing to forget others' faults.	Those who score high on FACTOR L are mistrustful, suspicious of people's actions and intentions, skeptical, and more self-indulgent and ego-involved.

FACTOR M

Low Scores Practical	**High Scores** Imaginative
Individuals who score low on this scale are concerned with the details of an issue or situation; they are governed by what is obvious, even to the point of being unimaginative	High scorers are thought involved, absent-minded, as it were, and imaginative; they don't want to be bothered with details.

FACTOR N

Low Scores Forthright, Genuine	**High Scores** Shrewd, Diplomatic
Low scorers on FACTOR N are more likely to be warm and honest, demonstrating a genuiness about themselves.	High scorers appear polished, shrewd, calculating, closed-minded and reserved, not easily influenced by the feelings of others.

FACTOR O

Low Scores Self-Assured, Secure	**High Scores** Self-Doubting, Apprehensive
A low score on the FACTOR O scale is typical of individuals who are relatively free of guilt, not easily disturbed or shaken by happenings, and secure in their ability to deal with difficulties.	Those who score high on FACTOR O are insecure and tend to be anxious, worried, and guilt-ridden. These individuals have high expectations of themselves and are overly concerned with handling difficulties.

FACTOR Q (1)

Low Scores
Conservative

Individuals scoring low on this factor are conservative, rather follow established traditions, are less tolerant of unconventional attitudes and ideas, and are not intellectually stimulated.

High Scores
Experimenting

High scorers, on the other hand, are more accepting of differences, yet critical and analytical. They are swayed more by intellect than by emotions.

FACTOR Q (2)

Low Scores
Group-oriented

Those who score low on this scale prefer the support of the group, feel more comfortable with decisions, and will seek group approval.

High Scores
Self-sufficient

High scorers tend to be independent, would rather act alone, and will disregard the opinions of others.

FACTOR Q (3)

Low Scores
Undisciplined

Low scorers on this factor appear lackadaisical, have very little regard for social demands, and are generally not assiduous; they also may show some difficulties in controlling their emotions and behavior.

High Scores
Self-disciplined

High scorers, however, are very diligent and have a great deal of emotional and behavioral control.

FACTOR Q (4)

Low Scores
Relaxed

Those who score low on this factor are low keyed and relaxed, having a composed, tranquil orientation toward life, and therefore may appear lazy and unmotivated.

High Scores
Tense, Driven

Those who score high, on the other hand, are tense, driven, and impatient. They are easily upset and have difficulty calming down once upset.

High scorers' high drive can enhance or inhibit performance, depending on how highly stimulated they are and how their excess energy is discharged.

REFERENCES

Cattell, R. B., Eber, H. W., and Tatsuoka, M. M. (1970). *Handbook for the Sixteen Personality Factor Questionnaire.* Champaign, IL: Institute for Personality and Ability Testing.

Krug, S. E. (1981). *Interpreting 16PF Profile Patterns.* Champaign, IL: Institute for Personality and Ability Testing.

Murphy, Lois. (1962). *Paths Toward Mastery.* New York: Basic Books.

Rhodes, W. A., and Brown, W. K. (eds.) (1991). *Why Some Children Succeed Despite the Odds.* New York: Praeger.

CHAPTER ONE

Surviving and Succeeding
After the Death of
Both Parents

For those who have had the good fortune of being raised by loving parents, even the thought of losing either of them in childhood can be traumatic. Most children at some point in their development experience this terrible thought or dream that their parents died. What happens to those children, less than 10 percent, who actually live through the nightmare? Does the death of a parent during childhood cause immediate and/or long-term effects? This is a question that theorists and researchers alike have pondered for years. Sigmund Freud, the father of psychoanalysis, is only one of many historic giants who postulated a relationship between childhood parental loss (including death) and psychological problems. Cognitive and behavioral theorists have also suggested that childhood parental death can have prolonged negative effects. Such theorizing has given way to a host of scientific investigations on the subject.

Most researchers and mental health professionals would agree that parental death will likely produce an immediate adverse reaction, but they are in much less agreement about the long-term adverse effects. Scientific investigations (e.g., Harris, Brown, and Bifulco, 1990; Tennant, 1988) have suggested a causal link between childhood parental death and various forms of adult psychopathology (i.e., depression, anxiety disorders, schizophrenia). Indicators of behavioral disturbances have also been linked to parental death (i.e., drug abuse, suicide, delinquency, and school dropout). Other investigations (e.g., Ragan and McGlashan, 1987; Thyer, Himle and Fischer, 1988) have failed to confirm a singular causal link between childhood parental death and specific or general forms of psychopathology. While many factors explain the mixed results, two stand out. (1) In a large number of the childhood parental death investigations, parental death has been treated as a subset of parental loss causing a confounding of results. However, parental loss may result from many factors, including separation, divorce, and abandonment. Recent research suggests that the reaction to parental loss may be mediated by the cause of the loss. (2) There is a lack of consistency in both the methodology and populations used in the various childhood parental death investigations, resulting in different conclusions regarding the effects of childhood parental death (see, e.g., Tennant, 1988; Zahner and Murphy, 1989).

Despite this inconsistency the preponderance of results do not support the belief that childhood parental death is the single cause of prolonged adverse effects. How a particular child responds to the death of a parent is probably the result of a number of factors, including the reaction of the surviving parent, the nature of familial support, family relations prior to the death and the child's personality characteristics.

Obviously, not all children suffer prolonged adverse reactions as a result of parental death. What factors seem to insulate a child from some of the reactions suggested in the literature? An extensive interview of an individual who suffered such a loss during childhood may provide us with some answers.

THE STORY OF CHAD

Chad, a cardiologist and father of three, says he has no real interest in learning why he turned out the way he did. He is a forward-thinking man, and to wonder about his childhood is to dwell on the past. But his life has been a success, and this is his story.

Losing both parents and lacking adult supervision and role models in the home would seem to condemn such children to hard-labor jobs or hard time in prison. Yet Chad and his brothers all have successful careers and family lives. Why did they succeed and do better in life than even members of their extended family who grew up with both parents?

Chad never knew his father, who died when Chad was only a few months old. Indeed, when he was growing up, Chad had very little in the way of a male role model. The lack of a father is in itself considered a hard but not insurmountable obstacle to a child's success. But then Chad's mother died when he was just 10 years old, and he and his brothers were left virtually to raise themselves.

Chad was the second of three sons born to his mother in a small Pennsylvania town outside of Philadelphia. His father joined the Navy to support his wife and two sons but was killed in the line of duty when Chad was just a baby. With a house, two sons, and a small monthly naval benefits check, Chad's mother took on the task of providing for her family. Not wanting her children to feel they had been cheated out of a father, she took special interest in all of their activities: she went to sporting events, she helped them with school work as they got older, and she supported them in any way she could.

Chad says he had seen pictures of his father, but he has no recollection of any real paternal influence in his mother's home. That is not to say there was never a man in the house. For several years after his father died, Chad's mother has a serious and exclusive relationship with another man. The two never married, even though they did have a son together. The man was in the Navy, and Chad remembers his family moving to Connecticut when he was three years old so his mother could be near this man's duty station when the baby was born.

Although Chad doesn't believe this man really abandoned his mother, the man never took an active role in her or her sons' lives. In fact, Chad can remember meeting him on only one occasion when he came over briefly one evening to fix the family's television set. Chad believes that his mother wanted to marry the father of her third child but that he had no interest in making a commitment to her. After the baby's birth, the family returned to their small Delaware County, Pennsylvania, home where they lived on the Navy checks.

Chad and his older brother were active boys who played both baseball and football from the time they were children through early adulthood. Although his mother feared he would be hurt playing such a rough game as football, she gave in to Chad's desires after he begged her on bended knee. She was the boys' number one fan—not only did she go to the games but she also was the secretary of Little League the year before her death.

Because his mother always lavished attention on Chad and his brothers, Chad says he never realized then that his family was underprivileged. It never occurred to him when he was young and his mother was alive that he was different from anyone else. He had his mother's full support, love, and understanding. Before Chad's tenth birthday, a lump was found in his mother's breast. Although she was gravely ill with cancer, she still tried to take part in her sons' lives.

Chad remembers his mother standing on the sideline at an autumn game, watching him play. During the action, a ball was thrown in her direction, and she was hit by one of the players as he attempted a catch. The boy ran into her cancerous chest. The blow caused her so much pain that she couldn't get up on her own and had to be taken to the hospital. From that time on, she was in and out of the hospital until she finally died there when Chad was in the fifth grade. Chad vividly remembers being told that his mother was dead. He was doing his homework, and his aunt came into the room to give him the news. He didn't grasp the concept of death and didn't understand why his aunt was crying so much. All he knew was that his mother wasn't coming home. Before she had gone into the hospital the last time, she had made plans to take Chad on trips. He recalls being very sad because now she wouldn't be able to play with him any more or carry out any of their plans.

The maternal aunt who had given Chad the news of his mother's death was named guardian for the children. But her husband had just left her, after she had announced she was pregnant with a fourth child, and she didn't know what to do. She was too devastated by her own troubles to take on responsibility for three more young lives. So while she was named guardian, she took no responsibility for caring for the three boys.

As for Chad's father's family, they were all Irish Catholics with big families, and they either could not or would not make room in their homes for three more children. In fact, although there were many members of both his mother's and his father's families, the only person to come forward to claim the children and take them was Chad's maternal grandmother. This small, strict Catholic woman moved into the house and tried to take over the boys' care, working very hard to keep an orderly household. She tried to keep her young grandsons in line by working with them on their manners and trying to make sure they all finished their homework. She was already 70 years old, however, when she came to live with the boys, and she suffered from arthritis.

Chad states that she did the best she could to keep up with them and to give them some guidance, but they did very little to help her. Indeed, they tried to get around her rules and go against her whenever they could. Even keeping up with the boys' nutritional needs was too much for her. Chad's grandmother did not drive, and she would walk to the store each day to buy food for the family, looking like a bag lady walking along the road, Chad recalls. He's sure she must have cooked meals, but all he and his brothers remember eating were cheese steak sandwiches. His grandmother would buy thinly sliced steak meat, fry it up, add some cheese, and put it all on some bread. Even Thanksgiving was celebrated with only the sandwiches to eat. Other holidays were not much more joyous. Chad remembers crying one Christmas Eve because he didn't have a family or a holiday to look forward to like the other children spoke about in school.

Sometimes the boys and their grandmother ran out of food altogether—usually when the grandmother was too weak or in too much pain to go to the store. On one such occasion, the boys started calling relatives to see if they could get some help. Of all the aunts and uncles called, only one, an uncle, came to their aid. Once he dropped off a few bags of food and then he left, never to be heard from again. Chad now looks back at his family's lack of helpfulness with anger and resentment. He believes that if he had been in the same situation as his aunts and uncles, he would have done more.

The boys started having problems, with each child's difficulty manifesting itself in a different way. Chad started spending time with some mildly delinquent children who lived in his neighborhood, devoting the evenings to drinking beer and finding mischief. As Chad didn't like the taste of beer, he would only pretend to drink most of it. In the rest of the activities, however, he was a full participant. The gang of boys would throw rocks through windows and loiter outside of stores until the owner chased them away. Some nights the police would come for them. The officers would always become angry with him because they thought he was lying when he said he had no parents to call. Usually the parents of one of his friends would also sign him out of jail, but invariably Chad was the last one to leave.

Surprisingly, despite all the turmoil in his life, Chad's academic stature remained good. While in elementary and junior high school, he always maintained high grades and was at the top of his class. He was the only one of the brothers who could make this claim.

Chad's younger brother took his mother's death harder than did the two older boys. Since his last name was different from theirs, he was not considered one of the brothers in school. Chad and his older brother had each other, but the younger brother was on his own. The year after his mother's death, the youngest brother stopped going to school and did not return for two years. Although Chad's older brother did remain in school, he was constantly in trouble. Because of all their difficulties, social workers were assigned to the boys. Chad describes them as the most obnoxious people he has ever met.

After reviewing the brothers' cases, the social worker said that the boys would be sent to an orphanage since they had no parents and certainly had no adequate adult supervision. Even though the boys did not have a clear concept of what life in an orphanage would be like, they didn't like the idea. After all, no orphanage they had ever heard of offered football, and both Chad and his brother wanted to continue playing. Finally, the boys told the social worker that they would not go; they said they would run away if they were forced into an orphanage. At this point the boys' guardian aunt stepped forward and said she would see that the boys were cared for properly. The boys were allowed to remain in their house, but not much changed.

Chad's older brother tried to take on the role of adult male figure in the house and would beat his brothers if they did something he didn't like. This caused many fights between the two older boys. Chad recalls that he and his older brother once fought so hard they broke all the furniture and the window in the front room of their house. When it was over, the two boys were covered with blood but had no serious injuries. Although Chad lost that battle, in a sense he won the war, for he had established that he would no longer sit quietly by and be bullied by his brother. Their relationship changed somewhat from then on. At least Chad did not go to school with any more brotherly bruises. The fight left the house a shambles, but it was hardly noticeable. With their grandmother unable to care for it and the teenage boys not about to make an effort, the house had fallen into gross disrepair.

Chad was embarrassed that the grass was never cut. The family had a push mower, but no one ever took the initiative to mow the lawn, and Grandmother never assigned the task. Paint had peeled off the exterior of the house, and the windows were caked with dirt. The house actually looked abandoned. Years later the house was sold and repaired—to the relief of the neighbors who then told him how happy they were that the house was finally being cleaned up. He imagines they were terribly annoyed at the state of the home, but none of them ever said anything at the time or came over to help.

After three years with the boys, at the end of Chad's eighth year in school, the grandmother suffered a major stroke that left her so disabled she had to go into a nursing home. The boys were allowed to remain in their home for a while longer as they waited to see if their grandmother would recover. When it became apparent that she would not return, it was decided that the boys could not be left alone to care for themselves. Thus, the three adolescent boys all went to live with the aunt who had been named their guardian, even though she was neither emotionally nor financially prepared to take on the extra burden. The aunt had remarried a man who had no children of his own, and being unaccustomed to being around teenage boys, he bullied them. Although Chad didn't mind because he was used to being pushed around, his older brother couldn't stand the man and decided to leave.

When Chad's older brother moved in with his paternal grandmother, Chad decided to go with him. It was the older brother's last year in high school and Chad's sophomore year. A football scholarship had already been offered to the oldest boy. The next year, he left for West Chester State College to play football, while Chad moved into his junior year in high school. At that time, however, their paternal grandmother had a stroke and was also institutionalized. Chad was left in the house alone. For the next two years, while Chad finished high school, he virtually lived alone and cared for himself. He says he didn't know who paid the bills, but that was not one of his worries. Because the Navy was still sending survivors' benefits, Chad assumed someone was taking care of expenses with that. Nor did he worry about the overall upkeep of this house. It was a large home in a well-kept neighborhood outside of Philadelphia. He took care of the interior, to a certain extent, but that was about it. Chad did not worry about money. He always had a paper route, and he would use that income for his pocket money. Although he had to wear a coat and tie to school (he went to a private Catholic institution), all he really needed was two ties and maybe two jackets, so clothing was not a problem. For food, he continued with the minute steaks or made sandwiches and did whatever grocery shopping he needed. Sometimes teachers and friends' parents would pity Chad and take him in for an evening or weekend to feed him. He remembers how fascinating it was to peer into other people's full refrigerators. It was a sight he had never seen before in any home he occupied. Suspecting that Chad's situation was not good (no one knew that he was actually living alone), his hosts would often feed him as much as possible and offer him sandwiches to take home. Chad was a greedy eater and a grateful guest. One of the coaches frequently invited him over to dinner; the coach's wife would tell Chad to help himself to whatever was in the refrigerator. Chad would gorge himself until he just couldn't eat any more; then the coach's wife would fix plates of food for him to take home.

Since Chad was now living ten miles from where he grew up, he had no friends in the immediate vicinity who could come visit. Although Chad dated and had girlfriends in high school, he never took them home because his house was such a mess. Many teenagers would probably have taken advantage of the situation and had wild parties and girls over all the time, Chad said, but he was too involved with the Catholic religion and too full of guilt to do something that could disgrace the family. Social services representatives would sometimes visit, but Chad's aunt would make up some story and they would leave him alone. They never offered help, he said, only pity. Chad didn't consider going back to live with his aunt. Several people, suspecting that he had a very different living situation, did offer some help. For example, one person from the school hired Chad to do some odd jobs and then paid him far more than the jobs were worth. But no one person took the responsibility to take care of him.

So Chad managed to survive on his own with what he had. He received some more money during this time when his family's house was sold. He received a third of the proceeds, with which he bought a car so that he could drive to school and sports practice. Chad played football and ran track during the school year and continued to train in the summer. There were several very good football players in the neighborhood who later became professional players. Chad would lift weights, run, and practice with them and with his brother who came home from college for the summer. He exercised whenever he wasn't working. Through a special needs-based program, Chad secured a job as a janitor at Bell Telephone for the summer, making enough money to put a little away for spending during the winter and to buy some new clothes for school.

Although Chad never did any homework assignments in high school, his marks were always high. He was named a scholar athlete, he was president of his class, and he was involved in many other social activities. He also received several sports awards, and a few small schools tried to recruit him to play football. But he knew that he wasn't good enough to become professional, and so he decided that going to school just to play football wasn't a great idea.

Entering his senior year in high school, Chad began sending

out applications to colleges. Because he didn't have much of a concept of schools, he just sent out applications to several different universities. Among the schools were West Chester State, where his brother was attending, Villanova, and Princeton. Chad's family and school counselor wanted him to go to Villanova, a good Catholic school, or West Chester State, where his brother was. His paternal grandmother was the one exception. On one visit to see her in the nursing home, she told Chad to go to Princeton because he could do better there than at the other colleges where he had been accepted. Chad himself preferred West Chester because during the school year he often drove up to visit his brother, see football games, and spend time on the campus. Chad wanted to play football; his brother was a good athlete, and Chad thought that West Chester was all that college could be. But one night, while Chad was visiting him at college, Chad's brother got drunk and told him not to be a "stupid shit" like he was and urged him to go to Princeton. Chad remembered his brother's anger, but it still wasn't enough of a reason. He finally chose Princeton because the school won the Ivy League football championship. Although Princeton offered no athletic scholarships, it paid most of Chad's tuition based on his financial need. Once he was in, payment of his tuition and fees was guaranteed as long as he kept his grades up.

College was a new world for Chad; he didn't even know that Princeton was a hard school. In his freshman year he declared physics as his major, started playing football, and then proceeded to treat college like high school. For his first physics test Chad studied the night before and got an A+, so he decided the class was easy and didn't go again. The night before the final, he got out his book and started to read. He flunked the final and just barely passed the course. The rest of his classes were about the same. He'd never received grades so low. Chad had never had to study before but had always enjoyed an intellectual challenge. The first real book he ever picked up to read was a biography of Dwight Eisenhower, which had belonged to his father. Chad was in fourth grade at the time and took about an hour to understand the first page, but he finished the book. He figured that Princeton was going to be the same way. Slowly,

Chad learned two things: the first was how to study, and the second was that he didn't like math.

Chad had liked the idea of medicine ever since his mother's illness; her doctors had treated young Chad like a real person, trying to explain to him what was happening. Chad saw medicine as a way to study the sciences without having to memorize a bunch of formulas. In addition, he realized he would be able to work with people and help them. He liked that idea, so he changed his major to biology. Princeton transformed Chad; before he went there, he had never considered becoming a doctor. Chad spent his first year at the school adjusting, but after that he noticed that students around him were planning to do all sorts of jobs he had never considered. These were people Chad didn't think were any smarter than he was. The Princeton attitude was that he could do whatever he wanted. Chad started to realize that he was smart and that he could be a doctor if he wanted. As he learned the rhythms of Princeton, his grades steadily improved. In his first freshmen semester he got all C's, and in the next semester he picked up two B's. By his junior year, he was making all A's, carrying a full load of classes while also playing football and lacrosse.

Chad also worked hard at making his summers productive. He spent the second summer in Boston. His roommate's father was a doctor in Boston and when he said he could get Chad a job working in the same hospital, Chad jumped at the offer. He worked as an orderly and loved the hospital. A new devotion to becoming a doctor sprang up in him that summer.

In the summer of his junior year, Chad wanted to work again in a hospital and this time he sought work in San Francisco where his roommates planned to spend the summer. Chad wrote to every one of the fifty hospitals in the San Francisco area in search of a summer job, and for his effort he received two replies. One was a very cold form-type letter, offering Chad a job programming computers, and the second was a long, rambling letter with bad grammar but a sincere message. The writer said he would really like to have Chad work with him for the summer. He didn't know how he would pay him, but he would find a way. Chad went to California.

Chad's new employer was from the Midwest and immediately

took a liking to Chad. For the first time in his life, Chad had a father figure. The man took Chad under his wing and took him home to meet his family. During this time Chad started applying to medical schools. He applied to many of the Pennsylvania schools because he was still a resident of the state and would have an edge over some other students.

During the early 1970s, many of Chad's past friends were going off to fight in Vietnam only to come back hooked on drugs. Meanwhile, Chad and half of his graduating class were applying to medical schools. Chad's employer/friend agreed to write letters of recommendation, but asked Chad why he hadn't applied to Harvard. Chad laughed, saying something to the effect that he would get into Harvard when cows flew, for his grades were not that good. This same attitude had prevented Chad from thinking he could be a doctor in the first place. The man persisted, however; he had gone to Harvard for a year and thought the school would be good for Chad. Eventually, Chad decided that all he had to lose was his application fee. Although Chad was eligible for a deferred fee, he said he preferred to borrow the money and pay the fee. He thought the free application would mark him as a needy candidate, maybe not up to par. As always, Chad did not want anyone's pity. Not only was he accepted, but he also received a scholarship.

The man in California was not Chad's only inspiration or father figure. In his sophomore year, Chad hurt his knee playing football, bringing his football career to an end. Because of Chad's condition, the university doctor spent a lot of time with the boy. Chad asked him to be his advisor. While most doctors at the university turned down such requests, this doctor decided it had merit. He became a source of inspiration to the young biology major. The doctor had left a thriving pediatric medical practice because it was no longer challenging and had come back to Princeton, his alma mater, to teach. His cut in pay must have been phenomenal, Chad thought, but the doctor was happy to be back in the school setting. He, too, encouraged Chad to apply to Harvard.

One day a week, the doctor would leave his Princeton University office and travel across the bridge to another section of town to run a clinic. It was in this clinic that Chad did research on methadone maintenance in his senior year at Princeton.

While attending Harvard for medical school Chad met his wife. She shared the house where he lived as a roommate in his third year of medical school. At the time both were involved with other people and they simply developed a friendship. Later, after she had moved out of the house, she and Chad kept in touch, calling each other about problems or making dates to get ice cream. By this time they had both ended their past relationships; even so a romance was slow to start. It was only over the course of the next year that they came to think of each other romantically.

Chad made it through medical school with a concentration in cardiology, and following graduation became a practitioner and an associate professor at a local medical school. During his tenure he has experimented with many different procedures, including angioplasty (an alternative procedure to major surgery designed to unclog arteries) which he brought to the hospital where he works. Chad enjoys his work, but says that by Harvard standards, he is a failure because he isn't a professor at an Ivy League school. Although he does not have to publish articles to maintain his professorship at the medical school, he is the author of 15 peer-reviewed articles on cardiology surgery.

Chad's wife has spent many of their years together trying to decipher his past. Talking to relatives and old school teachers as well as her husband are a few of the ways she has worked to piece his life together. From his old days of receiving only pity from people who knew about his situation, Chad is reluctant to talk about his past.

One piece of information that did not come as a surprise to her was Chad's love of a challenge and knowledge. Make something difficult, she said, and he will be drawn to it. He loves to work things out. For example, he has an extensive wine cellar because one day a friend showed him a crest on the label of a bottle and explained how the design showed where the wine came from. A different crest meant a different region. Realizing that studying wine, the different brands, flavors, and regions, involved an extensive learning process, he soon became fascinated. The continued challenge of learning something new is one of the reasons he chose medicine and cardiology in particular, his wife said. It offered a mental challenge.

Chad also loves precision and efficiency. Unable to sit idly, he manipulates his day to maximize efficiency. He wakes at the crack of dawn to take the dog for a walk, and as the dog walks, Chad reads the paper. He doesn't read just the headlines either; he reads every article, cover to cover. On his way to work, Chad has a teleconference with his associates; then he spends his day at the hospital and answers calls from his patients on his drive home. Chad's work week averages about 70 hours. His daily challenge is to press a 12-hour day into 10. Although he does not bring work home, he enters the house full of stress from keeping to his tight schedule. He relaxes by reading. His computer is programmed so that he can pay most of his bills with the press of a button. He thinks his computer was a great investment; not only does it free up some of his time, but it also was a challenge learning to use and program it.

Although there is a television in his house, it is in a room in the far reaches and is rarely used. Chad and his wife have three daughters and strictly monitor the time and type of television they watch, allowing them to watch only educational television. When he can, Chad spends his evenings with his children. He reads to them and plays games.

The only vice he admits to is flying. From the time he was a young man in high school, Chad wanted to fly planes. He almost went to the naval academy so that he could fly jets off aircraft carriers. When he became a doctor and had enough money to do so, Chad got his pilot's license. He has a commercial rating, which means he could fly commuter planes if he wished.

Because of his busy schedule, the importance he places on spending time with his family, and his wife's fear for his safety, Chad gets to fly only about once a month. On the weekends he flies, Chad wakes and switches on his computer. In the time it takes him to shower and dress, his computer is warmed up and giving him the weather forecast. He programs in his flight program for the day and sends it to the proper authorities. Then he is off. Chad says he really has nowhere to go when he flies; he just goes up and travels around. It is almost enough to satisfy his desire and just enough to keep his pilot license valid. One of his free-time reading projects is to catch up on the latest in aviation.

In all, he lives a very low-key life. His brothers have all become financially successful as well, and they keep up with each other, even though they all live in different parts of the country. Chad keeps his worldly goods fairly simple. His house is not a mansion; although he lives in a nice neighborhood, it certainly is not expensive or exclusive. For a man who wanted to be a priest in the fourth grade, a higher lifestyle would be too ostentatious.

Chad doesn't care or think much about the past, because that is where he wants to leave it. When he does think of it, he says, he gets mad only when he remembers that no one came forward to help him and his brothers. He does find it ironic that many of his relatives suddenly wanted to be part of his life after he became a doctor.

Guidance in his life did not come until he was well into college, so most of what he accomplished was through self-motivation. Although he does not keep up with many of his old delinquent friends of childhood, he knows that none of them went on to college. Chad's wife says that, after meeting his old friends at school reunions and talking to his old teachers, she is all the more amazed at all Chad has done. At one reunion, one of Chad's ex-teachers pulled her aside and commented on how surprised everyone was at his success. She was told that he was given every opportunity to fail. Chad says it was luck and hard work that helped him succeed rather than any special quality he possessed.

A SEARCH FOR SIGNIFICANT FACTORS

Undoubtedly, Chad has enjoyed tremendous personal and professional success, and from all appearances, he is happily married and a scholar in his profession. How does an individual who experienced the devastating loss of both parents achieve so much? Chad's level of success is even more amazing when we consider that he apparently received very little in the way of parental guidance after his parents' death.

Let us examine a couple of observations before we discuss

possible factors that may have helped Chad beat the odds. First, Chad, more so than the other successful individuals described in this book, did not consider himself different. He was not simply being modest: he genuinely did not want to be viewed as any different from the next guy. A sense of bitterness was evident when he described having to be treated differently. To this interviewer at least, it was obvious that Chad did not like being an "unfortunate." Being the beneficiary of food, grants, jobs, and the like, was degrading to him. One also detects Chad's sense of bitterness toward his surviving family for not giving him and his brothers more help.

Closely related to this initial point is Chad's desire to keep things that happened to him in his formative years in the past. He demonstrated no desire to explore his past experiences. It was his wife who made the initial contact with the authors; she was quite aware of Chad's background and was interested in how he had succeeded. Chad was totally disinterested in understanding many of his past experiences. On several occasions, he demonstrated serious "gaps" in recollection with no desire to explore them. For example, he did not know, nor did he care to know, who was paying his bills when he was living home alone. Chad's answer to many of the questions about his past were that he did not know or that he didn't think much about it. As a result of the "gaps," it is extremely difficult to put the pieces of his life together. Be that as it may, we will describe the characteristics that *seemed* salient.

The Mother's Influence

Chad was always sure of his mother's full support, love, and understanding. He described his mother as taking special interest in all his activities: helping with homework, attending all his sporting events, and so on. She was her boys' favorite fan.

While Chad described himself as obviously very poor—living off only his father's death benefits—Chad's mother was able to hide this fact from her children. Quite the contrary, he felt that she was lavish toward them. According to Chad, his mother did not want him to be considered any different from the other children in the neighborhood. From Chad's description, his mother provided the only "real" adult guidance he had.

Sporting Activities

Beginning at a young age, Chad was very active in several sporting leagues. He played organized baseball and football, and generally stayed in good physical shape by lifting weights and exercising. Being active in sports was supported not only by his mother but by the community as well. Characteristically, Chad's neighborhood encouraged youths to participate in sporting activities. Much has been written about the dominance of sporting activities in "small towns," and Chad's interest in sports was a product of that type of an influence. He continued excelling in sports even after his mother's death. Whether Chad's physical talent was man-made or God-given, he was good enough to win scholarships.

Influence of Benefactors: Known and Unknown

Chad received support (i.e., food, jobs, a needed signature to get out of jail) from his friends' parents, the coach's wife, and others. He must also have had an unknown benefactor, for someone was paying his bills and contributing to his growth in many other ways unknown to Chad. Expenses were probably associated with attending Catholic school or, at the minimum, exemption forms had to be completed; someone had to be fulfilling these and other obligations that a 12-year-old boy simply could not. Chad's inability to recall forbids the exploration of the who, why, and how of these unknown benefactors.

Social Status

While Chad resented being the object of someone's pity or being considered a "charity" case, as he describes it, he did benefit from his stature as an orphan. Almost begrudgingly, Chad admits receiving help through a special needs program. Undoubtedly, he received other assistance because of his social status and accompanying lack of resources, but Chad does not easily recognize or recall such assistance. He appears, both now and in his youth, to be a proud person determined to make it on his own.

Religious Influence

Despite Chad's arrest for minor delinquent offenses shortly after his mother's death, his conduct was greatly influenced by his religious instruction. He had numerous opportunities to adopt a life of crime and delinquency given his limited adult supervision, but his sense of religious guilt provided a restraint. On several occasions Chad mentioned the Catholic background of his immediate and extended family, emphasizing the family's religious orientation. While he did not mention that any specific religious instructions were discussed in his home, we can assume that a moral sense of "right and wrong" was established in the home and reinforced by the instructions received in the Catholic school he attended.

Chad stated that he did not have wild parties when he lived alone, not only because of his religious convictions, but also because he did not want to disgrace the family—the same family that had all but abandoned him and his brothers. Undoubtedly, allegiance to the family name shapes one's behavior and cannot easily be broken.

Personality Factors

Chad has always performed well in school. Obviously, his intellectual ability helped him excel academically. Matriculating at two of the most prestigious colleges and universities in the country, of course, attests to these abilities. Personality test scores administered as part of this investigation further support Chad's intellectual acumen. His personality test scores also suggest that he is serious, restrained, and cautiously introspective. He prefers working alone rather than in groups, and he is somewhat self-doubting and mistrustful. He scored in the average range on all other personality scales. A combination of scores, however, indicated that Chad ranks very high in creativity.

Generally, Chad's personality profile supports the information obtained in the extensive interview. He was open and honest in his responses in the interview as well as on the personality test. He wants to be considered an average guy, and, in many respects, personality tests support his view. However, he is very intelligent and is a hardworking, intense individual, who is constantly striving for perfection. It is believed that these latter personality traits contributed to Chad's beating the odds.

CHAPTER TWO

Growing Up in Foster Care

The need for children to live apart from their biological parents has existed since the infant Moses was set afloat in a basket to escape religious persecution and was ironically adopted by the very family that decreed the persecution. While religious persecution still exists, today children are more likely to be placed outside their homes because of parental dysfunction, especially mental illness, emotional and/or physical abuse, or neglect of children. Sometimes children are simply abandoned by their parents with no immediate relative available to care for them. Children who must live outside their homes are often placed in foster care.

The term *foster care*, as used in this book, refers to a number of out-of-home living arrangements, such as with foster parents, in small group homes, or in large institutions. Often children are placed in foster care temporarily, until the circumstances that precipitated the placement are rectified—for example, until parents receive counseling, become self-sufficient, or the child becomes manageable. Too often, however, children temporarily placed in foster care remain there for years. Some estimates indicate that children spend an average of three to five years in foster care, with some children experiencing multiple placements. The phrase "children adrift in foster care" has been used to describe the instability, uncertainty, and longevity of children's experience in foster care although placement was to be temporary and remedial (Maluccio, Fein, Hamilton, Klier, and Ward, 1980). For many children, rather than being temporary, foster care is an experience that carries them into their majority.

The social work field generally accepts the notion that a child's developmental needs are best served if the child is raised in a permanent living arrangement, preferably with biological parents. Furthermore, if placement outside the home becomes necessary, if at all possible it should be only temporary. Placement decisions should be guided by a concern for the health and well-being of the child. When the needs of the children are taken into consideration, placement preferably should be with a relative, and, if this is not possible, the child should be placed in the least restricted environment. "Children adrift in foster care" contradicts the wisdom of using foster care and is a problem that plagues the foster care delivery system.

The Adoption Assistance and Child Welfare Act of 1980 (Public Law 96–272) was enacted to help establish permanency planning in children's lives and to reduce the incidence of children remaining in foster care longer than necessary. Permanency planning has thus become a critical part of case management for children in foster care. While there are varying definitions of permanency planning, Fein, Maluccio, Hamilton, and Ward (1983) state that permanency planning essentially embodies a number of key features:

- A philosophy highlighting the value of rearing children in a family setting, preferably their biological families.

- A theoretical framework stressing that stability and continuity of relationships promote children's growth and functioning.

- A program based on systematic planning within specified time frames for children placed (or at risk of placement) in foster care.

- A sense of mutual respect and a spirit of active collaboration among child welfare personnel, lawyers, judges, and others working with children and their parents.

- A case management method emphasizing specific practice strategies such as early delineation of long-term plans for the child, legal processes, case reviews, contracting, and decision making, along with active participation of parents in the helping process. (pp. 486–487)

Some experts (Fein, Maluccio, Hamilton, and Ward, 1983) stress the need for permanent planning for foster care children because our child welfare system has usually been ineffective in either preventing children from entering care or helping them to reunite with their biological families. Unfortunately, in most instances responsibility for preventing the placement of children in foster care and ensuring that they are quickly returned home falls on the shoulders of social workers who are often underqualified, overworked, and underpaid.

What happens to children who are raised in foster care? While there are conflicting data on the effects of foster care placement— some suggesting that children become worse, and others suggesting that children function at preplacement levels or better— high rates of delinquency, adult criminality, and violent criminal behavior are apparently associated with children in foster care (Widom, 1991). Regarding separation, Papalia and Olds (1986) suggest:

Most mothers and fathers form attachments with their children from a very early age, and these attachments exert a major influence on the children's physical, intellectual, and personality development. When these attachments are interfered with, either due to the child's separation from his or her parents or due to a hurtful, rather than a helpful, relationship with them, the consequences can be grave. (p. 164)

The separation associated with foster care placement is usually very painful, not only for the children involved, but for their parents as well. Even children who are placed in foster care because of physical abuse and neglect find the separation from parents very painful. Children who are physically separated from their parents are often unable to separate themselves emotionally because of a belief that the placement is only temporary. These children are unable to establish meaningful relationships with foster parents, often feeling that to do so would be to betray their parents. A typical scenario is one in which a child is separated from his or her parents and is placed to stay in foster care without any real chance of returning home; as a result, the child is deprived of a real opportunity for normal emotional development. The normal fears and anxieties, the lack of trust, and the feeling of insecurity stimulated by separation from parents become major adjustment problems for children placed in foster care and often lead to behavior problems.

The frequency and severity of adjustment problems are exacerbated when the child experiences multiple foster care placements. However, some children manage to rebound from this potentially devastating blow to become successful, well-adjusted adults. Why? Barbara is just one example of an individual succeeding under foster care placement despite the odds.

THE CASE OF BARBARA

In 1990 Barbara started work on a program designed to show young people the many options they have in their lives other than drugs and alcohol. She took to the project with such zeal that she almost neglected her own family while she worked 14-hour days to get everything started. She says she worked so hard because, thinking back to her own childhood, she realized her life could have turned out much worse than it did had someone not intervened to make her aware of her options.

Today, Barbara lives in a large house that she and her husband built in a nice, slightly expensive neighborhood. But Barbara vividly remembers days in her adolescence when she would get off the school bus at the end of the day and not know where she would sleep that night, or whether her family's furniture would be out on the curb again. Between the ages of 11 and 13, Barbara and her brother moved at least eight different times with their mother. But sometimes, when their mother moved to other states to find work, she would leave them in other people's care for months at a time and ultimately for years. From the ages of 13 to 21, when Barbara got her own apartment, having foster parents and living in a foster home became a way of life for her.

It has taken years for Barbara to overcome the bitterness as well as the fear and anxiety that were the hallmarks of her childhood. Strangely, however, Barbara remembers her early childhood as a time of happiness. She was born in a small town near Rocky Mount, North Carolina. Her earliest memory is of a time before she was 3 years old, when her father took her to a parade along the main street in town. She remembers sitting on his shoulders and the dress she wore. Her memory clouds after the parade. Her parents divorced soon after, and her mother, Delores, moved to Norfolk, Virginia, taking Barbara along. Her father, a tall, handsome, accomplished baseball player who had a chance at playing professional ball, came to Norfolk a few months later. He stopped only long enough to pick up young Barbara and take her back to North Carolina, where she lived with her maternal grandparents.

Barbara doesn't know why her father listened to her mother's parents, but she thinks their influence was a major reason behind her parents' breakup. Barbara's parents had married when they were very young, and Delores was already pregnant with Barbara. During those first years of marriage, they lived with Delores's parents. Delores's mother had her own ideas of how the young couple should live, and, unfortunately, these ideas often conflicted with her daughter's ideas. Years later, Barbara would look back and conclude that her father was the only man her mother had ever loved, although she had had many boyfriends before she died. Barbara also thinks that their marriage never had a chance of survival because they lived in her grandparents' house.

After Barbara's father brought her back to North Carolina, he took no further responsibility for her care. As a result, Barbara has no sense of ever having had a father. Rather than stay with her at her grandparents' house, her father moved out and started another family with another woman. Barbara saw him only on special occasions.

Life for Barbara at her grandparents' house was hard but not altogether unpleasant. The area was predominantly agricultural, and Barbara remembers sometimes being taken out of school to work in the fields. She was often punished because her fear of worms in the cotton fields kept her from making very much money as a cotton picker. She also worked in the vegetable garden and helped with meals while her grandmother worked in the tobacco factory.

Her grandfather worked on the farm during the week and at getting drunk on the weekends. She remembers him getting dressed up on the weekends and going out to town. Small arguments sometimes erupted between the grandparents, but Barbara doesn't remember anything very serious. Although she isn't sure exactly what the problem was about, Barbara learned that some stigma was attached to being who she was. On the school bus one day, another student hit her in the head simply because of who her family was. She didn't dwell on what the other children said then, she says, and she doesn't worry about it now. Her life was pleasant enough since she had many relatives to play with when she was young.

Her grandparents' house was small, but it was home, she said. Besides Barbara, several young cousins also shared the three-bedroom house. The children slept three to a bed. Her most lasting memories of those years are of the outhouse, the water pump, wearing shoes only to church, eating banana ice cream, riding a bicycle down the lane, and visits from her mother. "Dressed like a movie star and looking beautiful" is how Barbara describes her mother when she would come to visit. Barbara was always proud of how her mother looked and sad when she would leave to go back to the city.

Barbara had cousins in Baltimore whom she would visit and who would come to visit her in North Carolina. She always felt a little inferior to her fast-talking, shoe-wearing city cousins and dreamed of the day when she would go to live in the city. She thought it must be heaven there. Barbara often wrote to ask her mother when she could come live with her. She received no reply to that question for many years.

Because she was Black, Barbara attended a Black school with Black teachers. It was there that she began to feel she would like to be a teacher. The images of the teachers at the school and the special interest two of them showed in Barbara will stay with her forever, she says. The two teachers, Mrs. Bridges and Mrs. Matheson, would often take Barbara to their homes and on special outings. Their encouragement made her want to learn more and more; they often told her to finish her education and to go to college. The rest of Barbara's immediate family was relatively uneducated. Barbara worked for the approval of the two teachers as hard as she could.

When Barbara was seven, another child came to live at her grandparents' house. It was Barbara's half-brother who had been born in Baltimore where her mother was living at that time. He was a healthy baby boy, and Barbara helped care for him. Playing the role of his mother would become second nature to her in the years to come. At the age of three, Barbara's brother was hit by a car. The accident caused severe head injuries and broke both the boy's arms and legs. He was temporarily blinded and would have learning problems for the rest of his life. It was a tragedy, but Barbara learned how to adapt. She had become very good at adapting.

At the age of 11, Barbara's prayers were finally answered when her mother came for a visit and left with her two children in tow. "I felt I had arrived," Barbara said about the first time she came to Baltimore to live with her mother. When asked as an adult why she believes her mother finally decided after eight years to claim her children, Barbara answers honestly that she believes it was because of money. Her mother, who had always sent the grandparents money to care for the children, apparently decided that if she had to send money, she might as well care for them herself and keep the money. The apartment where Delores first took her children to live was located in a nice section of town. Barbara says there was a window seat and a feeling of space about the whole place. She loved it. But the apartment was too expensive for Delores to manage, and the family stayed there only briefly. They then lived in a string of increasingly smaller apartments in worse and worse sections of town.

When Delores moved her children to Baltimore, she was working as a barmaid and for a short while made enough money to live on and even to allow for a few luxuries. But she had very little time to spend with her children; a hurried dinner with their mother before she had to rush off to the bar was a real treat to the children because they so rarely spent time with her. Since her mother was working in the afternoons, Barbara would have to hurry home from school each day to take care of her brother. She oversaw life at home during the evenings and made sure her school work was completed, even though it sometimes had to be done by the light of the streetlamp because the apartment's electricity had been turned off when Delores failed to pay the electricity bills.

Barbara has no recollection of her mother having any real involvement with her during this time or really any time in her life. The little security that Barbara had felt by just being with her mother soon began to disappear with the frequent moves, the homes without electricity, and the occasional complete lack of food. Barbara blames bad choices relative to alcohol, men, and money for her mother's decline. On one occasion when her mother got drunk, Barbara remembers her mother bringing home a man one night and the next morning hearing her cursing loudly as she woke to realize the man had left and taken all her money with him. Delores's bouts with drunkenness became more frequent during this time. As she fell deeper and deeper into alcoholism, Barbara became increasingly uncertain about their daily existence.

Delores's smoking was yet another problem. She often fell asleep with a lit cigarette in her hand, once causing a fire in the family's home. So Barbara made it a habit to awaken at night to check on her mother and to make sure it never happened again.

A few months and several moves after Barbara came to live with her mother, a man joined the family. "I just woke up one day and he was there, and he stayed," she said in describing the suddenness of the new person's arrival. The extra adult added no stability to Barbara's situation. Her mother still worked, but the man did not. Violent arguments often erupted between the two. Barbara sat in the room she shared with her brother and wondered every night if that would be the night that her mother and the newcomer would kill each other, for their fights were often harsh and brutal. Barbara recalls her mother once chasing the man around the apartment as she beat him on the head with her shoe.

With the increase in drinking and other problems, Delores lost her job and the family went on welfare to survive. Being poor was one thing, Barbara thought, but being on welfare was a complete disgrace. She didn't want any of the other students in school or neighbors at home to know just how bad life had become. Delores soon found another job, however. The job was in New York State, near the Canadian border, and she worked as a live-in maid in a mansion. Because Delores could not take the children with her, Barbara and her brother were sent to live with an aunt.

If Barbara had thought she was in Heaven when she first arrived in Baltimore, she thought she was in Hell now. Barbara describes her aunt as the laziest woman she has ever known. Barbara had just turned 12 and shared a room with two female cousins. The aunt had five children of her own in a big house she had just built in a nice neighborhood. Her husband had been killed recently in an industrial accident, and it was the insurance money that paid the bills.

Barbara was charged with caring for her aunt's baby, as well as cooking most of the meals and doing much of the cleaning. The baby slept with its mother, but Barbara remembers having to get up in the middle of the night to change the baby's diaper as the mother slept only inches away.

The move was very difficult for Barbara, even though she had already moved several times in the last year. She says she was suddenly dumped in someone else's house, where her mother was not often spoken of fondly because she frequently did not send the money she had promised the aunt for watching the children. Barbara's position was precarious, to say the least. Delores would come for short visits during her children's six-month stay with the aunt. The visits lasted no more than two hours and often occurred when Delores was on her way out of town after spending a weekend in the city.

Barbara remembers going to school without any breakfast and without any money to buy lunch. To top things off, a male neighbor took an amorous interest in her. She became so frightened and disgusted with the whole situation that she called her mother and told her she would run away and take her brother if she did not return for them. "I told her we were not laundry that could be dropped off and left somewhere," Barbara said.

Delores returned for her children; she was pregnant and had lost her job in the mansion anyway. The three of them found an apartment in another section of town, which meant that Barbara had to change schools for the third time that year. Delores was five or six months pregnant when her former live-in boy-friend in New York City asked Delores to move her family into a nice place he'd found for them there. Pulling her children and their few possessions together, Delores had her family on the next bus to New York. The "nice place" Delores's boyfriend had was actually an old, dirty, small hotel room. Delores and her family rarely left it. The boyfriend did not live with them but brought them food during his visits.

Sometimes, the boyfriend didn't bring food to the room. Once Barbara was sent out to the corner store to buy some meat and cheese so the family wouldn't starve. The trip was traumatic. Not only was Barbara sent out into the big city on her own, but a vagrant tried to molest her. Every night she prayed that she would not have to go out alone again.

The New York life last only a few months and then, for reasons Barbara does not know, the family was on the bus again, headed back to Baltimore. The new baby was expected any day and Barbara wondered where they would find a place for it in the tiny basement apartment her mother had found for them. Space was what she remembered about the first Baltimore apartment, and the lack of it was what distinguished the new place. This was the worst of all the places she had ever lived. It was filthy, and Delores, who had always been a very tidy woman before she started drinking, did nothing to clean the small rooms. She would be there only a few weeks though before moving yet again.

The baby, a girl, was born in Baltimore in a taxi soon after the family's arrival there. Barbara and her brother stayed with rel-atives while her mother went to the hospital.

The next apartment was with the old boyfriend on the third floor of a building. They stayed there for only a few months before another move came. But this move, in the winter of 1962, was different from all the others. Delores was again going to another state to work, without the children. Instead of sending the small family to a relative though, this time she found what she described to Barbara as a nice Christian couple for the chil-dren. Mr. and Mrs. Smith were an older couple with grown children. Neither Barbara nor the Smiths knew it at the time, but the temporary situation would become permanent, and the

Smiths would become the parents Barbara had never known before.

The Smith home was indeed a Christian home; the children went to church every night and took part in a prayer session with the adults every day from the moment they moved in. Barbara thought that her mother had taken advantage of the nice couple's generosity by asking them to take the children, but she didn't know what to do. The house where they lived wasn't huge, but it was large enough that, for the first time in her thirteen years, Barbara didn't have to sleep with anyone. It was a row house with a fence and a garden and marble stairs in the vestibule, Barbara says. It was sparkling clean, and everyone was given chores to keep it that way during the week. On weekends the whole house was scrubbed from top to bottom; no one escaped helping. Barbara learned discipline and structure in this house, she says.

Barbara was there for a year when she overheard the Smiths talking about Delores's not sending money for the children's care for some time. Barbara also missed her mother more than usual. She had sent many letters to Delores's supposed address, but they had all been returned unopened. Barbara had received no word from her mother for several months, and no one knew where she might be.

Later they discovered that she had lost her job as a maid because she was pregnant and had not bothered to tell anyone. The Smiths, not knowing Delores's whereabouts and financially unable to care for the three children alone, decided to go to the state authorities.

Barbara, her brother, and her baby sister were to be put up for adoption. Everyone said the baby would have no problem finding a home, but Barbara's age and her brother's learning disabilities made them virtually unadoptable. Being a truly soft-hearted couple who could not stand to see the children torn apart, the Smiths asked the state to name them permanent foster parents. The Smiths request was granted, and Barbara was at least given a home she wouldn't have to leave. Her life started to change almost immediately.

Barbara says she never felt like an outsider in the Smith home. Although she knew that the Smith children didn't think it was appropriate that their parents were going to raise a new family at their age, they never showed any resentment to Barbara or her brother or sister. Barbara remembers her first Christmas in the Smith home, when she, her brother, and sister received presents just like everyone else. She was touched to be treated like one of the family. Christmas with her mother had not always been so festive. Mother Smith took great pains to let each child know he or she was special. There were cakes and special meals for birthdays, and they were encouraged to excel in their academic and personal lives. Under the care and love of Mother and Father Smith, Barbara began to blossom. She again had time to study and do well in school. She received several awards and scholarships, and her teachers encouraged her to continue her education. Barbara again began to dream of going to college.

Mother Smith believed in discipline and a strong Christian background. When Barbara got her first job at the age of 16, Mother Smith started teaching her priorities and responsibility with money—something her mother had never known. Her foster mother explained to her the difference between the necessities of life and the luxuries. Most things which weren't directly needed to sustain life fell into the category of luxury, Barbara learned. From each paycheck, some went to tithe the church, some to Mother Smith, and some into a savings account. Barbara could spend the rest of the money on whatever she wanted, with Mother Smith's approval. Barbara is grateful for the first financial lessons Mother Smith gave her. She admits that as an adolescent she didn't like having to turn over or save a large amount of her money, but in this way she learned the value of money and what to expect if she were out on her own.

Barbara was, and still is, a workaholic. She said that when she was younger she strove so hard at everything because she desperately wanted approval and reassurance; she does it today simply because that is what she's used to.

Her life was not completely serene, despite the stability she had achieved. Barbara still wanted to be part of her mother's life and have her mother as part of hers. Legally, she was not allowed to have any contact with her mother, but all the same she sent birthday and Mother's Day cards, as well as letters to her mother on a regular basis. Mother Smith neither encouraged or discouraged her letter writing. Barbara also had a visit with her mother, even though that, too, was against the foster care rules. It came during a time when Barbara was feeling over-worked and unhappy in the Smith home—basic adolescent emotions, she said. She told Mother Smith that she would be happier with her mother and wanted to visit her. Mother Smith let 16-year-old Barbara go to New York City to see her mother.

The weekend started off badly. No one came to meet her bus into the city, and Barbara had to figure out how to get to Staten Island, where her mother was living. When Barbara arrived, she had a meal with her mother before Delores left for work. Barbara was left to care for her two half-brothers, who had been born since her mother left the other three children in Baltimore. Barbara didn't see much of her mother that weekend. The old ways of working late and sleeping-in in the morning were still very much a part of her mother's life, it seemed, as was her drinking habit.

At the end of the weekend, Delores had the day off and went to the bus station to see her daughter off. But this nice gesture was also ill-fated. Her mother was so drunk that day that she fell into a plate glass window, and while the window didn't break, Delores developed a huge bump and had trouble walking. Whether it was from the alcohol or the fall Barbara never knew. Back in Baltimore, Barbara knew she lived in the better of her two worlds, and yet she would yearn for her mother's approval and love for many years to come.

Having done well in high school, Barbara received a scholarship to go to college and entered the University of Maryland in Baltimore County in September 1966. Although her foster parents didn't understand her desire to go to college and thought she should get a job, they respected her decision. Since the Smiths didn't want Barbara to live on campus, she woke up early every morning to take the bus to school and walked a mile from the bus stop to get to her classes.

In addition to her studies, Barbara attended church with her family every night and on weekends. She studied before and after the service and at the same time held a part-time job. This schedule was, of course, too much for her. After being placed on academic probation in her second year of school, she left

school and took a job in a bank. Barbara says that while she
made good money she longed to go back to school, feeling a
fire for education within her. She wrote an impassioned letter
to the school, explaining why the school should take her back,
and vowing that she would do better and that she had a goal.
The school did reinstate her, and Barbara was true to her word.
She had felt herself a failure when she left school, and today
she is very happy that she didn't let that initial failure stop her.

Majoring in English with a minor in education, Barbara graduated in 1972. Her natural parents were invited to both her high
school and college graduations, but neither came. In fact, Barbara saw her father only twice after she left North Carolina. One
meeting took place when Barbara was in her late teens and she
was in North Carolina to attend her grandfather's funeral. Someone told her her father was at the corner store so Barbara went
down to see him. He asked for a hug, which she gave him, but
conversation was strained, at best. Not surprisingly, she felt that
she was talking with a stranger. She stayed only five or ten
minutes and then left. The next time she saw him was at his
funeral, and she was 23.

Barbara got married in 1973. Although she had dated often in
college, she hadn't been involved with anyone before she met
her husband. Her years of uncertainty with her mother had
made her very self-reliant and introspective. She reasoned that,
having invested so much energy in her mother, she didn't have
any to give to a relationship with another person. In addition,
seeing her mother depend on men so many times and be disappointed, Barbara had become wary of men and learned to
depend only on herself because she was the only person she
was sure of. Even today, at the age of 43, Barbara says that when
there is a problem, her first reaction is to withdraw into herself,
an instinct that she must continually fight.

Barbara was drawn to her husband because of his stability,
she says. He didn't drink, which was important to her after
watching alcohol destroy her mother's life. He had also paid his
way through school by himself, and he had ambition. His stea-
diness and reliability gradually produced a trust in Barbara
which has lasted throughout their marriage. They dated for a
full two years before deciding to marry. Barbara's foster father,

who was really the only father Barbara had ever known, gave her away at the wedding. Sadly, Mother Smith had died the year before.

Barbara worked in public relations at the university until 1976, when she left to have her son. Instead of going back to work, Barbara started studying toward getting her master's degree. With several stops while she worked teaching English and in the Admissions Office at Morgan State University, Barbara finished her degree in December 1989.

In 1987 Barbara's mother died of pneumonia in New York City. She had been seeing a married man for years who just dropped her off at the hospital when she became ill. Barbara went to New York to make arrangements for transporting her mother's body to Baltimore for the funeral. In her reflections on her mother, Barbara contemplated how her mother had wasted her life, and she remembered the mother of her early childhood days and how over the years the spark in her mother's eyes had died. After the funeral, Barbara says she remembers sitting in a room with her mother's married boyfriend who, instead of speaking words of consolation, announced that her mother owed him $300. Barbara was so angry at the man, who for her epitomized the bad decisions her mother had made, that she actually felt like cursing him, but she fought back the urge.

Although Barbara had maintained a relationship with her mother until the end, their relationship had changed over the years. They actually had several screaming sessions, as old guilts and accusations surfaced, with the result that Barbara finally decided she had to make a break if she were to recover from her own emotional scars. The culminating event in their break came at Christmas time in Barbara's thirty-third year, when she was celebrating with her husband and son and her mother called. Delores said she was at the bus station with Barbara's two half-brothers and asked Barbara to come get them. Barbara decided it was time she stopped being a co-dependent for her mother and declined to get her. Delores refused to speak to her for months afterward and when she finally did, they had a grand argument. "It was a chance to air all our problems", Barbara said. The problems remained, but Delores and Barbara came to an understanding.

Barbara says she never felt that her mother was really a mother to her; rather, she was more like an older sister whom Barbara needed to care for. Barbara's younger sister doesn't remember her mother at all, and Barbara's brother hasn't forgiven Delores for the emotional heartache he feels to this day. Barbara's brother and sister both turn to her when they have a problem. It is a pattern established long ago, when all three were children.

The years of cleaning up after the emotional messes her mother had left made Barbara bitter and resentful. She denied these feelings and placed no blame on her mother for years, she said, but eventually she had to face the fact that the woman who gave birth to her was not a good mother.

Living with foster parents was at first traumatic because it required acknowledging that her mother couldn't or wouldn't care for her children. As a result, Barbara started attaching herself to teachers and counselors and found herself working extra hard for recognition that she was worthy of love and caring. Her foster family did love her, and their love was her saving grace. Their caring and encouragement brought her through many rough times. With so many people caring about her, it's not surprising that she chose to become somebody, she says. "You don't disappoint family. It's important to have other people who think what you do is important," Barbara said.

Barbara defines her success as more than financial, professional, or even marital. For her, success is being at peace with her past, with her mother, and with herself. Healing her emotional scars is the true success of her troubled life, and that began when she entered a real Christian family and accepted Jesus Christ. Through the years, Barbara maintains, she had to decide that she couldn't change the past, only herself. She has learned the valuable lesson that she wasn't responsible for what happened to her when she was young, but that she is responsible for what she does. Barbara says it took her until her thirty-third year to completely overcome her bitterness and realize her own self-worth.

With her husband and two children, Barbara lives in a large house that they built near the Chesapeake Bay, a home that is far more than she ever dreamed of as a child. She has returned to teaching college English, for that was her first love. Barbara emphasizes over and over that her life could have turned out a disaster and she wants everyone to know they have options.

A SEARCH FOR SIGNIFICANT FACTORS

Barbara became a successful college teacher despite the turbulent years of uncertainty during middle childhood when she did not know where or with whom she would be living. As suggested earlier, professionals have not reached a consensus with respect to the outcome of foster care placement. For Barbara, foster care placement was an unqualified success. What factors were significant in her foster care placement experience?

Influence of Teachers

Barbara specifically remembers the encouragement, support, and special favor given her by two of her primary school teachers. They encouraged her academic efforts, offered college as a future option for her, and generally fostered her love of learning. Apparently, these teachers developed a relationship with Barbara that extended beyond the classroom. They took her to their homes and included her in family outings. As a result of the relationship kindled by the teachers both in and out of school, they were able to serve as role models for Barbara, as she incorporated the teachers' goals and dreams and worked hard at her studies to please them.

Early Experience as Caretaker

As a child growing up in a house where her mother did not always behave as a responsible adult, Barbara was initially forced to assume caretaking responsibilities for herself and eventually for her siblings. In Barbara's case, Delores's child neglect led to Barbara's early development of caretaking skills and responsible behaviors that are expected of adults. For example, Barbara found herself managing the home, taking care of her brother, supervising her own school work, and looking in on Delores late at night. Interestingly, as an adult Barbara could have become as irresponsible as her mother had been, but instead of copying her mother's actions she disdained many of her mother's actions and consciously attempted to behave differently. This approach is particularly evident in Barbara's orientation toward men. Observing the destructive nature of her mother's dependency on men, she was determined not to be like her mother in that regard.

The Foster Parents' Influence

Undoubtedly, the Smiths had a tremendous impact on Barbara's development. Granting the Smiths permanent custody of Barbara gave her a sense of stability that had an immediate positive effect on her life. Barbara felt that the Smiths totally accepted her into their home, introducing her and her siblings to a family life that she had never known. Barbara credits the Smiths for her sense of discipline, structure, and financial responsibility. As a Christian couple, they provided love, caring, and encouragement that Barbara calls "her saving grace." Barbara worked for the Smiths' approval as they encouraged her in her studies and her personal endeavors. She believes the Smiths are responsible for the hardworking behavior and attitude that she exhibits today.

Religious Influence

Barbara did not mention religion as an important element in her life prior to coming to live with the Smiths. However, religious activities instantly became a dominant part of her life, as the family engaged in daily prayer and church attendance. Even her homework took a back seat to church activities, as Barbara was required to complete her school work between church services.

Personality Factors

Barbara's personality scores suggest that she is a sensitive, warm, and easygoing person. In addition, she can be described as a venturesome person who enjoys social contact, and yet is not easily influenced. She apparently has high moral standards that keep her conduct consistent with societal expectations. In line with the interview data, Barbara's personality scores indicated that she has a strong desire to meet her responsibilities and could excel in leadership positions.

From Barbara's interview, we could easily ascertain that she has a strong and longstanding desire to please others and to excel in school. Personality test scores indicate above-average mental skills to succeed in the academic area, possibly suggesting why Barbara was drawn to school teachers. That is, Barbara needed approval, and she had the mental skills to succeed in school, and did so, which evoked the approval of her teachers.

Because Barbara's earliest childhood recollection was a happy one, we cannot dismiss the possibility that her natural parents created a resilient child. It is also possible that Barbara was born with a stress-resistant personality. Our profile of Barbara cannot definitively determine whether her current level of success is a result of parental experience prior to foster care, personality factors, the foster care experience itself, or a combination of these or other factors. The current profile, however, provides some insights into the potentially significant factors associated with successful foster care experience. Further research and analysis emphasizing these factors can help us determine the actual impact.

CHAPTER THREE

Growing Up in a Single, Female-Headed Household

Patrick Moynihan's report in 1965 on the condition of the Black family epitomizes the pathological perspective that is most often employed in assessing the Black family. Is it destined for extinction, or was Moynihan exaggerating the picture? The Moynihan report has provoked a great deal of criticism and debate.

The Black family in America is indeed in trouble. Government can help prevent the free-fall, but if Black families are to be saved, Blacks themselves are going to have to do more to save themselves. We need only look at this statistic: approximately one in four Black males ages 20 to 29 are behind bars, on parole, or on probation, compared with 1 in 16 White and 1 in 10 Hispanic males (Wilder, 1991, p. 99).

Some twenty-six years later, Virginia's governor L. Douglas Wilder, the first Black man in U.S. history to be elected governor, shares Moynihan's pronouncement of doom for the African American family. The statistics used to support numerous claims that the Black family and the Black child, in particular, are in trouble are startling:

Black children, compared to White children, are:

twice as likely to
• die in the first year of life
• be suspended from school or suffer corporal punishment

three times as likely to
• live in a female-headed household
• be placed in an educable mentally retarded class
• be murdered between the ages of 15 and 19 years

four times as likely to
• be murdered before one year of age or as a teenager
• be incarcerated between 15 and 19 years of age

twelve times as likely to
• live with a parent who never married. (Edelman, 1987)

   Too often, the problems associated with the Black family have been attributed, in full or in part, to the large number of Black children reared in single, female-headed households. This family lifestyle is said to be pathological and dysfunctional in comparison to the two-parent middle-class White family, which is often considered the norm. Recent reports (Herbert, 1984) have heightened public awareness of and sensitivity to Black, single, female-headed households. These reports portray the Black family as doomed because of the high percentage of female-headed families. Census data support the observation that a significantly larger proportion of Blacks than Whites are reared in single, female-headed households (Edelman, 1987; Fine and Schwebel, 1991). More children are born to Black unmarried than to married females. According to recent statistics (*Delaware Health Statistics*, 1992), during the years 1985–1990 about 28 percent of all U.S. births were to single mothers, while the percentage of Black single mothers was about 62 percent. This has not always been the case: "Until recently, two-parent families have been the black family norm, despite great publicity given to black female-headed families. It is only in the 1980s that the majority of black infants have been born to unmarried mothers—the culmination of a trend that began in the 1950s" (Edelman, 1987, p. 7).
   Although large numbers of White children are also reared in single-parent households, their status is usually the result of parental divorce and separation rather than out-of-wedlock pregnancy, as is often the case with Black children. According to

Fine and Schwebel (1991), how children adjust in a single-parent family may depend on the cause for the single-parenthood status. Some research seems to support the perspective that the Black, single, female-headed household is pathological, while other research does not. According to Fine, Schwebel, and Myers (1987), conflicting findings on the pathological nature of the single-parent Black family, as often presented in the literature, can be understood and explained, and are dependent on the researcher's underlying assumptions and values.

Fine and Schwebel (1991) provide an insightful repudiation of the Black single-parent family as pathological. The pathological orientation of the literature has overshadowed the fact that many single Black females are raising children who are not delinquents, who graduate from school, who are highly motivated, and who become quite successful. As suggested by Edelman, we could learn a lot from those single Black mothers who have done a valiant job in raising their children. In an attempt to identify factors that make the Black, single, female-headed home functional rather than pathological, the current chapter provides an in-depth look at one of the countless Black children who have succeeded under these circumstances.

THE CASE OF DAVID

Many people believe that a Black child growing up in a home with no father has more than his or her fair share of disadvantages. How could such a child be expected to succeed in the economic or emotional world? David grew up in such a home, but it never crossed his mind that he was disadvantaged. In fact, given his situation, he felt he could do nothing but succeed.

David, the first child of four, was born near Charleston, South Carolina, in the days before integration and the civil rights movement. His house lacked indoor plumbing as did many homes of the era, and his closet was not packed with clothing. David's neighborhood was a poor one, but it was "upper class" compared to some of the surrounding neighborhoods. He attended the country school with the other neighborhood children. David didn't know who his father was until he was in his twenties; so David decided one day to ask his mother, and she gave him the name. His father was a married man when he got David's mother pregnant, so he acknowledged neither his mistress nor their son. Perhaps that is why David's mother never asked the father for any help. David believed there were two reasons that he was not stigmatized and shamed as an illegitimate child. First, his mother had finished high school and was 21 years old when David was born. In the town where David grew up, it was not a disgrace to have a child out of wedlock, as long as the mother was not a teenage high school dropout. "People figured she was old enough to lead her own life," David said. But second and undoubtedly most important, David's maternal grandmother was a pillar and a leader in their small community.

He describes his mother in the years of his youth as an attractive woman and a partygoer. The third of seven children, she was the recalcitrant and difficult member of the family. Although she lived in her mother's home before and during her pregnancy, when David was born she rented the house next door and moved in, desiring some independence but not wanting to be far from her family. His mother's house was small— one story with an outhouse. David believes his mother moved there because she figured that, with a child, she was an adult and should run her own life. She dated heavily, so she was most often out of the house for the evening. David said that many men came to the house to court his mother, but none of them was there long enough to take on a fatherly role. Her job kept her out of the house daily from about 8 A.M. to 5 P.M., so David was cared for by an aunt or his grandmother. His mother was a good mother when she was at home, David said, but she wasn't home very often.

David's mother and grandmother were not very close and often disagreed. His mother was the stubborn member of the family who smoked and drank in opposition to her mother's wishes and teachings. Still, David was always cared for and fed by either his mother or his grandmother. He remembers his childhood as very happy. David knew his family was poor, but he didn't think about it much because they were so resourceful. Thus, he never worried where his next meal was going to come from. At Christmas, David would receive a toy gun and a holster so he could play "bang bang shoot 'em up," and that was all he wanted. But even during childhood David says he knew that someday he would have more. His grandmother played a major role in David's upbringing, taking him to church every Sunday while his mother stayed home.

David's mother was very protective of her son because he suffered from asthma and was sometimes hospitalized with attacks that would cause him to pass out from lack of oxygen. Sporting activities such as football were forbidden for David out of fear that they would trigger an asthma attack. He was, in fact, very sports minded. He was intrigued with the world of sports, and he wished he could become more involved. At first he watched many games, but, because he wasn't allowed to play as a child, he soon turned to learning. As he got older he tended to look at the "jocks" as stupid; "football players always had trouble in school," he said.

When David was 4 years old, his mother gave birth to a baby girl. The baby's father took a part in her life but did not express much interest in David. Even so, David doesn't remember being jealous of the fatherly attention his sister received. Two years later another sister was born, and then another two years after her. David was 8 years old and took it upon himself to help care for his two new sisters. For two years he assumed the role of father for the young ones; he made sure they were changed, fed, and happy. His sisters all had different fathers, none of whom ever married David's mother. With each of the previous two pregnancies, she wouldn't reveal who fathered her baby, and, as far as David could determine, she sought no financial or emotional help from the men. David remembers his baby sisters as the most beautiful children he had ever seen. Unknown to the family, both girls were born with heart defects, and they died within a year of each other when David was 10. He was devastated by the loss of his sisters and felt responsible for their deaths because he couldn't help them. For years their deaths left him feeling hollow.

Shortly after the deaths of her two youngest children, David's mother decided to move to New York City alone. He and his sister waved goodbye and moved in with their maternal grandmother. His mother equated the city with opportunity and a good time; the north was the promised land. The move from his mother's home to his grandmother's was not very traumatic for the two children inasmuch as his mother was not home very often and he had already been raised mostly by his grandmother. It was her values and rules by which he was already living. David thought of his mother much as if she were an older sister who occasionally cared for him. Therefore, when she left, he did not blame her, feel abandoned, or become angry. He now believes that she did what she thought was best for her children and for herself. Because he was still grieving for his sisters at the time, his mother's departure was only a small event in his life.

The guiding force in David's life was his grandmother. Taking over the total care of her grandchildren did not significantly change her life, for she had been caring for the children as if they were her own since their birth. She owned the home where she lived and raised her children and grandchildren. Her husband had died eight years before David was born, when David's mother was 13. After the death of her husband, David's grandmother vowed not to remarry because remarriage would have gone against her strong religious beliefs. She was a large woman in stature and had equally high standing in her community. In her household, everyone went to church each Sunday unless afflicted with a grave illness. Sundays also brought a big family dinner to which the minister was invited. The grandmother, having great strength of both body and character, set the pace for the family. "She had the power of God behind her," David said. "There was nothing she couldn't overcome." She believed in being morally right and was not afraid to share her philosophy with others. David grew up with her admonitions that he would have to pay for any wrongdoing in which he took part. "What you do in the dark will come out in the light," she used to tell him. She taught David that he controlled his own destiny and that he would have to work to succeed. He said it was her words and teachings that completely excluded any thoughts of criminal activity from his mind.

His grandmother also hired herself out as domestic help, working very hard to provide for her family. There wasn't money for a lot of frivolous extras. Meals might not always include a large meat dish, but no one wanted for food in her household.

Nine people shared grandmother's two-story, three-bedroom wooden clapboard home. One of David's uncles left every evening to sleep in a retired nurse's home, and David's aunt worked nights providing in-home care for an elderly woman. David shared a room with two other uncles when they were sleeping at home. But these uncles were no more a guiding parental force for David than his mother had been; in fact, both uncles were closer in age to David than to his parents.

David's neighborhood was small and rural, with everyone knowing everyone else and looking out for each other. David grew up with many friends his own age in the town. Although his situation as a member of a single-parent home with no knowledge of his father's identity was not unique, there weren't many who shared his status. Even so, no child or adult ever said anything derogatory to him about it or made him feel the slightest stigma when he was young, he said. He believes that it was his grandmother's moral resolve that shielded him and prevented other people from saying insulting things about him. His summers were spent in much carefree play. While he was responsible for certain household chores, when they were finished he had most of the day free to wander. David and his friends would chase each other and hold shoot-outs with their toy guns. Marbles was another favorite game, and when David could get away with it, he and his friends would play an easy game of football. Sometimes a group of boys would sneak off to the local pond where they would strip naked and swim. They all knew that if they were caught they would face severe punishment, but the heat and laziness of the summer days seemed to make the stolen swim worth the risk.

When David was a little older, he was also given the job of helping his great-uncle with his firewood business. Since the uncle was old and unable to do most of the work, David and one of his younger uncles would end up cutting and stacking all the wood. The uncle would sell the wood for $20 a cord, and of that amount David would receive $2. He thought the situation was unfair, but because it was family and his grandmother had told him to do it, he kept quiet and did the work. Asthma attacks, which became more and more infrequent as he got older, were the only excuse for not working for his uncle.

During the winter, David attended a small country school with shared classrooms and few students. Always performing very well in school and considered the smart member of his family, he had an image to maintain. He therefore studied hard in school and always managed to make A's and B's. He could not stand the thought of letting his grandmother down because she had faith in his ability, and he was going to justify her faith. But David also had an inner drive that he felt from the time he was very young. He always felt the compulsion to do better in whatever he attempted. Success was something he was sure he would achieve, in all avenues he took.

In the sixth grade, David was placed in a classroom with a male teacher, and his academic life took flight. Although the teacher had a wife and young children of his own, he took David under his wing and gave him special attention. David would help him in the classroom by writing grades in the grade book and cleaning up. The teacher, in turn, opened David's eyes to the world of literature. David had always been a reader, but under this teacher's care, he was exposed to Greek mythology, Charles Dickens, and other classics. David began taking extra books out of the library to read, and, with money he earned from helping his great-uncle, he began buying paperback editions of certain books so he could read them as many times as he wanted.

The teacher had a profound belief in education and hard work as the keys to success. David recalls that this teacher spoke with great dignity about the education of the Black man and the opportunities available to him. Education, he maintained, was the solution to breaking away from poverty and racial stereotypes. David and his teacher became very close; David often went home with the teacher to have dinner with his family. Since the teacher's own son was just a toddler, David's close relationship with the teacher never interfered with family relationships. Under his tutelage, David became less timid about speaking out and expressing his opinions. Although David had always been a good student, with his teacher's help he was motivated to be even better. His first great love of reading came from this teacher. To this day David still loves Charles Dickens, his special teacher's favorite author. David finished sixth grade as class salutatorian. Of all the disappointments in his childhood, the one he says he remembers most is not his lack of a father, but his forgetting his whole speech as he got up to make his salutatorian address. Even though he and his teacher shared many confidences, theirs was never a father-son relationship. Rather, the teacher was more like a caring friend than a parent, serving as David's mentor and helping him in his search for success.

"I think I was the son he needed at the time," David said. Even in the summers and on weekends and holidays, he and his teacher spent time together or corresponded. Every summer, the teacher stayed with his family at the beach, where he worked as a cook in a hotel. When David reached his teen years, the teacher took the boy with him and got him a summer job. He continued his friendship and daily encounters with his teacher for about four years. In that time, David's drive and determination to go to college were strengthened by the goals his mentor had set for him. "I think he was grooming me to take over. To come back to teach."

As the star pupil in the little country school, David enjoyed a privileged standing among the students. He was given the run of the school and helped teachers with their work. But when he reached high school age, his aunt decided that his intelligence was being wasted in the small school. She decided he should go to the city school in Charleston where he could get a better education. David was expected to go to college, and the courses in the city served as better preparation for higher education. Upon transferring to the city school, David's whole life changed. Whereas he had been the "king of the hill" at the little country school, he was completely unknown at the city school. His new classmates numbered more than the entire population of his old school.

The daily commute was also a big change. David used to walk to school, but now he faced a 25-mile commute each way every day. Since his aunt lived in the city and his grandmother worked there, he wasn't totally alone. The new environment, however, was like moving into a new country, so David suffered considerable culture shock. His relationship with his old teacher waned as David's time was eaten up with the bus rides to school and the extra studying he did to keep up at the new school. His grades dropped slightly when he first moved to the new school, but he was determined to do well and regain his former academic excellence as well as some status in the school. Therefore, he worked long hours studying, and finally he pulled his grades up and made a name for himself as a good student in Charleston. He had other reasons to maintain a good grade average: one was his overriding desire not to disappoint his grandmother; another was the knowledge that he would need scholarships to go to college because his family would be unable to pay tuition. He knew he could do it. He was not the first member of his family to go to college, for his aunt already had a degree. The goal, though in reach, would require a lot of diligence.

In retrospect, David says that going to the city school was a good move for him. Had he stayed in the country school, he probably would have been admitted to a college but would not have been so well prepared. The larger school offered courses in science and math that were unavailable in the rural education system. But most important, going to the larger school taught David to be competitive. At the country school, he did well without much work, but in the city, David had to work hard to stay on top. Toward the end of his senior year, his mother returned from New York. She had undergone dramatic changes in her life. Once a carefree party girl, she was now married and settled down to country life. She had also stopped drinking, smoking, and cursing and began attending church on a regular basis. She continues her virtuous lifestyle to the present. But to David his mother's return was as insignificant as her leaving had been. She had sent money and visited during her years in the city, but she had never been a mother figure to him. So her return and her changes didn't made a great difference to his already set life. Furthermore, her new husband was not ready to be a father to a teenage boy. Nor did David expect the man to take a paternal interest in him. He had lived this long without a father and didn't feel he needed one at this point.

Fortunately, David kept up his studies, finished up at the city school with honors, and prepared for college. As a member of the honors class, just before graduation he was called to the school counselor's office for a discussion about college. The counselor had given each student a list of colleges where he thought the students' talents would be best developed. On the list was Morehouse College, in which David did become interested, but he wasn't sure he wanted to go there right away. It wasn't until the president of Morehouse spoke at David's high school graduation that David became sold on the school. He applied and was accepted but had applied too late to be eligible for financial aid for that year. When a local college offered him a scholarship, he decided to attend for a year—until he was eligible for financial aid at Morehouse. David spent his first year of college at Allen College in South Carolina and went to Morehouse College the next year to major in physical education and minor in journalism, all while holding down a job to help pay for his education. He lived and ate on campus. He estimates a year at school cost about $2,000 complete. While that isn't much money by today's standards, it was a fortune for David. He received both scholarships and financial aid and worked at whatever odd jobs he could find.

College, like the city school, was uncharted territory for David. For the first time, he was away from home for an extended period. He did not travel home often, and he stayed at school or traveled to a job in another city during the summers to work. The internal pressure to succeed increased for David as he found himself in classes with valedictorians and salutatorians from all over the country. His worries increased as he watched one student—whom he knew to be intelligent—flunk out of school. Returning to Charleston a failure was David's greatest fear. He knew many people were counting on him, believing in him. He knew that the shame of having to return home without his degree would kill him.

During the summer when he was away at college, David learned one lesson that he would never forget. He didn't learn it in class, but it helped him in class because it reinforced his priorities to finish school and make a better life for himself. During his sophomore year David didn't bother looking for a summer job because, since he'd always found jobs easily, he figured he could find one whenever he chose to. But to his dismay, he found that all the desirable positions—in local offices, at the college, in local stores—were long gone by the time he started looking, after school ended. David had to take a job laying underground cable for a power company, which was horribly dirty, hot, hard manual labor, work hardly appropriate for a "college man." The experience sorely wounded his ego, putting him at the receiving end of merciless ribbing from his schoolmates and coworkers. To make matters worse, the nearest bus stop was located right next to Spelman College for women. Unable to bear the thought of any of those beautiful, refined, intelligent coeds seeing or smelling him as he returned home from a grueling day's work, he would get off the bus three stops earlier and walk a roundabout route home to avoid passing anywhere near Spelman.

Besides teaching David that he never, ever wanted to do this type of work again, this experience forever etched in his mind to go after what he wanted with a vengeance, and to do so early. Never again was he caught so unprepared. For the two summers after his underground work experience, David worked in Washington, D.C., at a job his cousin found for him. Although it still wasn't an office job (he worked moving inventory in a warehouse), it paid a very good salary that helped immensely in meeting his ever-rising college costs. College was a happy time for David; he worked hard and he did well, making the Dean's list every year. He also joined a fraternity and made friends that he would keep forever. He graduated with a degree in physical education and a dream of becoming a sports writer. Morehouse had been filled with students from all over the country, many of whom had come from privileged backgrounds with many monetary and educational advantages.

As he watched his freshman class of 550 students dwindle to the 169 students who graduated, David, from a poor rural background—without benefit of a father or even his biological mother in a sense—pondered the amazing thought that he had managed to graduate with honors. Much of his success came from the competitiveness of the college, he said. Most of his classes were small, with fifteen or fewer students, so he always had to be prepared when he came to class, because there was no way the professor would not notice him. Moreover, David didn't seek to be merely prepared; he wanted to be the best and to know the work better than anyone else in his class. He still feels that being prepared and "better than the next guy" is very important.

To his old mentor's disappointment, David did not return to his small town to become a teacher. One thing David knew was that he didn't want to be a teacher. Job opportunities for a Black man in the South in the late 1960s and early 1970s were quite limited. Since he had no hope of finding a job back home in South Carolina, he never returned there to live. However, David occasionally returned to visit his grandmother, who had become an invalid after a robe she was wearing was set ablaze by a space heater, and she was burned over much of her body. She was confined to a bed and developed arthritis. The woman David had remembered as big and powerful, and the guiding force in his life, was now small and withered. He remains very bitter about her situation; after all she had done for others, he believed she deserved better than her fate. She died a few years later, in pain.

David's first job was as a sportswriter for a major newspaper in North Carolina, and he loved it. Although he had job offers from as far north as New England, David chose North Carolina for its proximity to home. It was here that he met his wife. They married in 1975 and had their first child three years later; David, who never had one himself, was now a father. He admits he was a little nervous but took to the job of "daddy" with the same drive and enthusiasm with which he approached any new challenge. David's son is now entering adolescence and, although he has to cope with the usual parent-teen conflicts, he and his son are very close. This is the only time David has ever felt he might have missed something by not having a father. He says he has nothing and no one to look back on as an example of what a father should be. David says he can never know what it's like to have a father. "I don't know what that feels like," he said. "I only know the relationship I have with my son. It's wonderful to hear him say, 'Dad.'"

David has also instilled in his son the same love of learning he had as he was growing up. David knows the importance of education and stresses that to his son. David's son has taken to learning very well indeed and is in advanced classes in school;

he also takes extra classes on subjects in which he has an interest in the summer. David believes that environment is very important in determining how a person grows up, and as an example he points to his own upbringing. He grew up in an atmosphere where he couldn't be a failure; he couldn't disappoint his grandmother who showed great interest in which he was doing. He also says he had a lot of self-drive, which came from being poor in a small town. He did not want to grow up to work all week just to get the weekend to drink. To avoid that trap, he knew he must continue his education.

On the job front, David left his newspaper job to take a position as assistant public relations director of a North Carolina college, where he also earned a master's degree in journalism. He had since taken a job as director of public relations for another college in another state. Financially, David is doing as well as he had hoped. He said his goals were to have enough clothes to change his suit every day and enough money to provide a good home for his family. David has everything he wanted. Even as a child he never doubted he would succeed. He had drive and he refused to be a failure. He says that he took a lot of blows in his youth, but he never let them stop him. A person can't let things get him down.

A SEARCH FOR SIGNIFICANT FACTORS

Obviously, as shown in David's case, being raised in a Black, single female-headed household is not tantamount to being sentenced to a life of poverty, hopelessness, and a host of other social ills. Intuitively, most of us know that, but because the negative factors associated with being raised in such a household are so often emphasized, we almost automatically feel sorry for the individual who is not raised in the "normal" two-parent home. And if the household is headed by a single Black female, we tend to feel the situation is even more hopeless. The authors are not suggesting that one lifestyle is superior to the other, but that certain factors do contribute to a successful outcome for some individuals raised in the Black, single female-headed household. Knowing what these factors are will contribute more to helping people "beat the odds" and become healthy adults than knowing what factors contribute to failure in these situations.

Several factors were significant in David's success. The factors identified here are hypotheses—"best guesses." They are offered as potential significantly contributing factors that merit further investigation for their usefulness in helping others in similar circumstances.

David Was Not Stigmatized by the Term *Illegitimate Child*

David never considered himself illegitimate. In listening to his opinions on the subject, we get the impression that he hated the concept when growing up and currently views it with even greater disdain. Being an offspring of a single mother who dropped out of school and being stigmatized as an illegitimate child was a fate David abhorred, for such a negative label presumably contributed to poor self-esteem for some of David's peers. As noted earlier, David did not suffer from the potential negative consequences of such an identification. David believed he averted this stigma because of his grandmother's status in the community, his mother's age when David was born, and her graduation from high school.

Grandmother's Influence

David mentioned that his grandmother's high status in the community carried a degree of respect from others as well as responsibility on his part. One can only speculate on how David's mother as a youth had reacted to being raised by a mother so valued by the community. In any event, for his part David perceived his grandmother's status as contributing positively to his development. Living close to and later with his grandmother, receiving religious instruction, physical, emotional comfort, and the like, as acknowledged by him, contributed to a standard of moral development that served David well in his youth and to this day still serves as an underlying orientation toward life. His grandmother's impact on him was so powerful that he could not allow himself to let her down. Whether it was staying out of trouble or fulfilling academic goals, Grandmother's influence always seemed to guide his behavior.

Multigenerational Family and Neighborhood Influence

David was raised in a multigenerational family environment. Aunts, uncles, and grandparents lived in the same house, which provided, among other things, more eyes to watch over children and more money to support the household. In addition, he described his neighborhood as one where "everybody knew everyone else and looked out for each other." Much has been written about the positive influence these two factors have in the Black community; David echoes the sentiment.

David's Physical Condition

David's asthma restricted his activities, undoubtedly keeping him home more than other children and leading him to choose academics as a means of enjoyment, self-concept formation, and self-esteem enhancement. He obviously had the mental capability to excel in school, and being forced, as it were, by his asthma to pursue such a course allowed David to fully develop his innate intellectual ability. We can only speculate whether he would have succeeded in academics had he been allowed to spend most of his time in sports activities or unsupervised play.

His Mentor's Influence

David's teacher served as a role model/mentor who reinforced David's budding love of reading, introducing him to a whole new world of literature which David found exciting and compelling. The more David read, the more he loved to read. The teacher also stressed that working hard to reach one's goals was important and that education was the key to breaking away from poverty and racial stereotypes.

David emphasized that the teacher did not function in a fatherly role, although the teacher did seem to behave, in many ways, as a father would. David stated that he was the son the teacher needed at the time and that the teacher treated him like part of the family, indicating that the teacher may have perceived himself in a paternal role but that David seemed to resist perceiving the teacher as such. David was more comfortable placing the teacher in a caring friend's role. Along this line, interestingly, David refused to acknowledge any other male functioning in the fatherly role.

Personality Factors

David described himself as having a self-motivating drive "from the beginning." Whether this drive was created by experiences beyond David's recollection or was a result of inborn personality factors cannot be determined. David also verbalized a self-affirming orientation toward life. As described by McHolland (1976), a self-affirming person is one who is self-confident, has positive and realistic feelings and attitudes about oneself, knows one's strengths and weaknesses, and generally feels worthwhile and satisfied with one's life.

The personality test indicates that David is an extremely sensitive, warm, and easygoing person. He responded to test items in an open and honest manner and showed no sign that he wanted to present an overly positive image of himself. Indeed, David's personality profile indicates that he tends to be genuine and forthright. He is practical, preferring to work independently and usually making decisions on his own rather than through a group. David's personality profile complements his current occupation, which may, in part, explain why he is so self-affirming. Generally, David appears happy and well adjusted and is by no means emotionally and/or socially scarred.

CHAPTER FOUR

Succeeding Despite Parental Divorce

Parental separation and divorce occur at an alarmingly high rate in the United States. In particular, a dramatic increase in the divorce rate took place between 1965 and 1979. While the rate declined slightly between 1979 and 1984 (Hernandez, 1988) and appears to have leveled off since then, the rate is still relatively high. Some experts estimate that 40 to 50 percent of American families with children will divorce and that many of these children will spend an average of five years in a single-parent home. The length of time residing in a single-parent home is much higher for Blacks than for other racial groups. It is also estimated that 80 percent of divorced men and 75 percent of divorced women will remarry and that 47 percent of their second marriages will end in divorce. These data suggest that many children will experience separation and divorce twice.

Such situations are, of course, extremely stressful to children and parents alike. Adults who divorce are more likely to experience a major psychiatric disorder: depression, suicide, and alcoholism are among the many psychological problems found to be associated with divorce. Difficulties at work, in interpersonal relationships, and parenting problems also plague adults experiencing divorce. Children may manifest the stressful effects of divorce in ways similar to adults; they may experience depression, engage in self-injurious behavior including suicide, and become involved in substance abuse. A multitude of school problems may result, including fighting, stealing, frequent tardiness and absenteeism, poor academic achievement, and even school dropout. Even delinquency has also been associated with divorce.

Children's reactions to divorce vary depending on their developmental levels, but very little is known about the effects of divorce on infants. However, young children experience a tremendous amount of fear, anxiety, and even anger as a result of divorce. They may feel abandoned by the parents, believe that they are the cause of the separation, and retain hopes that the parents will reunite. Research suggests that children who were very young when their parents divorced ten years later recall little of the initial pain and suffering they experienced at the time of the divorce. On the other hand, those children who were older or in adolescence when their parents divorced readily recall the earlier distressing emotions and find themselves affected by the divorce ten years later. Even though divorce is usually stressful for children, not all children suffer the negative emotional effects suggested by the literature. A great deal of diversity exists in children's responses to separation and divorce.

Following the initial responses to the crisis period in their parents' divorce and remarriage, some children exhibit remarkable resiliency and in the long term may actually be enhanced by coping with these transitions; others suffer sustained developmental delays or disruptions; still others appear to adapt well in the early stages of family reorganization but show delayed effects that emerge at a later time, especially adolescence. (Hetherington, Stanley-Hagan, and Anderson, 1989, p. 304)

Since not all children are seriously harmed by separation and divorce, what factors appear to be related to an adequate adjustment for children experiencing these changes in family structure? Research suggests that adequate adjustment is related to the child's personality characteristics, parental conflict before and after the divorce and/or separation, the quality of the new family structure, and resources and support systems. Separation and divorce per se, which may result in single parenthood and/ or remarriage—a change in the family structure—are no longer considered by most researchers as deviant and destructive in and of themselves. Waln experienced a great deal of stress as a result of his parents' divorce; however, he was able to demonstrate remarkable resilience to this disturbing change in his family structure. His case is presented to gain insight into factors underlying his resiliency.

THE CASE OF WALN

Waln today is a tall, impressive, self-confident, successful man in his late forties who has a doctorate of philosophy in anthropology and is director of a foundation to help delinquent youth. It is hard to imagine the depths into which his life fell more than thirty-five years ago, when he was institutionalized in a psychiatric hospital and a school for delinquent boys following the divorce of his parents and the alienation of his father from the family. But the institutionalizations were only the culmination of many problems Waln faced and created during the long years of his childhood.

Waln's earliest home memories begin when he was about 4½ years old and his family lived in a small Pennsylvania town. Those memories aren't of familial bliss, but of heated arguments between his parents and of his father's frequent, extended absences. Looking back on his life, Waln says he can't remember ever feeling any real affection or love from his father. He admits his father was never openly cruel; he was just uncaring. For example, after one argument between his parents, young Waln told them he wanted to live somewhere else, so his father drove him to the door of the county orphanage and told him he could get out. Waln's father sometimes attempted to play ball with his son, but with two jobs to support his family and what Waln terms a very self-centered personality, a solid father/son relationship never developed.

When Waln was 11, after the birth of two more children, his father finally moved out of the house for good. With his father gone, the in-house fighting between his parents was over. Waln was allowed to visit his father every Sunday, visits he describes as tense at best. The time before and after the visits was filled with the awful words his mother had to say about his father. The time during the visits was no better as the father would send as many venomous barbs in the mother's direction as he could. As an added complication, Waln's mother insisted that the children were unclean when they returned home. She made them strip down and take a hot bath, scrubbing them with disinfectant solutions to clean away all the filth she said they had accumulated from their father's house. Waln now understands that his mother was suffering from an obsessive-compulsive personality disorder that caused her to be overly concerned about dirt and germs.

Waln doesn't remember when the disorder started, or if it added to the unrest between his parents or was caused by it. All Waln knows is that he felt the guilt of a child who thinks he or she must have done something very wrong for his parents to have argued so much, and then to separate. In truth, many of their arguments had been about Waln and how his mother overprotected him. She believed he was different from other children because he had suffered rheumatic fever and anemia as a baby, so she constantly kept him in her sight as a way of preventing a recurrence of either dangerous illness.

Waln's father called him a "mama's boy" and at one point even made him fight three neighborhood children in an effort to toughen him up. Waln remembers the beating he got from the other children, but no comfort from his father as he stood battered and bruised afterward.

After two years of visiting his father on Sundays, Waln stopped going. On his last visit, his father introduced Waln to another teenage boy. Waln's father explained that he wanted to marry the boy's mother and make the boy his son. As he explained his plans to his children, he hugged the other boy— affection Waln wanted from his father but never got. It was on that Sunday that Waln decided his relationship with his father was finished. He never received assurances from his father to the contrary. Even years later, as more trouble began to mount in Waln's life, social workers asked his father to take a more active family role, but he would not.

His father's departure was not Waln's only problem. Without

her husband's income, Waln's mother was forced to move her family into her parents' small home, where she shared one room with her three children. Waln and his younger brother shared one small bed, while his mother and baby sister slept in the other. With the new living arrangements and Waln's growing feelings of guilt and self-doubt, his grades started to fall. He barely passed seventh grade. His body started twitching with the inner turmoil he felt, and he began to physically lash out at people and objects. Soon after his behavior problems began, at age 12, Waln faced what he considered a devastating rejection. His mother took him to a Lutheran home for orphaned, neglected, and dependent children. Although Waln cried and begged her not to leave him, his mother said it would be the best thing to help him with his problems. Until this first "institutionalization," Waln never questioned his mother's love, only her strange cleaning behavior. With placement in the Lutheran home though, he now had a new doubt—the doubt that his mother really cared for or wanted him.

Waln spent only two weeks in the home. During that time he went out of his way to avoid everyone. He hid in closets, under sheets, on hills, and in empty classrooms. After winning the initial wrestling match to declare dominance in the boys' dorm room, the other children in the home left him to himself. He ate and lived alone. At the end of the first week Waln was given a pass to walk into town. He figured this pass was his perfect chance to run away to the prairie. He had visions of owning a stallion and living in peace with no one to bother or hurt him any more. Thinking his plan outstanding, he called his mother to tell her about it. She said she wanted to come say good-bye in person but instead alerted the home's officials, who sent people out to recapture Waln. A week later, the home called Waln's mother to come pick him up. The home's director termed Waln "antisocial" and stated that the home had nothing to offer him. Looking back, Waln feels that the stay at the Lutheran home could have been a turning point in his life if he had remained there. He believes it was the inconsistencies in discipline, rules, and affection at home that helped lead to his confusion and lack of a steady emotional base on which he could stand to face the world. Waln's faith in his mother had been shattered when she took him to the Lutheran home. Their relationship would never regain its old closeness, as he waited for the next time he would be sent away.

Other changes began taking place in the household soon after Waln came back from the children's home. For the first time in her life, his mother had to find a job to help support her family. It was not an easy task for a woman who had barely graduated with few skills from high school before becoming pregnant and marrying Waln's father. After months of searching, she finally took a job at a local YWCA as an assistant athletic director. The pay wasn't very good, but it provided enough to keep the family going and some benefits as well: the children could spend time with their mother while she worked. But that little family time was short lived. After a year, she left the Y to take a better paying job at a dentist's office. Her hours were long and varied. The children sometimes went to the office to see their mother, but they were soon informed that a dentist's waiting room was not a playroom for three children.

But it wasn't just the job eating away at the time his mother had to spend with her children. When she was at home, she was often tired or sick, suffering from many ailments that often caused her to be hospitalized, miss work, and spend much time under medication. Waln's grandparents, 65 and 70 years old, tried to fill the parental void for the children, but they were too old to offer any real emotional support to the young children on a consistent basis. In addition, health problems began to plague more of the family. The grandfather suffered from leukemia, and the grandmother had heart problems. On top of all his other problems, Waln also developed severe acne which covered his face, neck, and back with sores and pustules.

The burden of caring for his brother and sister increasingly fell on 13-year-old Waln's reluctant shoulders. Although his grandparents tried to keep a positive outlook, he could feel them slipping away. A fear of being left totally alone, without any of the adults he cared for, caused him to act even more negatively. Guilt and frustration from his inability to hold on to the people he loved only added to his inner turmoil.

Waln's grandmother, a deeply religious woman, soon lost patience. She started to berate Waln for his behavior, often telling him she thought he was "in league with the devil" and that his acne was "the evil in his body trying to get out." Waln started to blame all the problems at home on himself and thus tried to spend less and less time there. Home wasn't the only place that he was avoiding. He began lying about illnesses to stay home from school, and he would often skip school if an excuse didn't work. Waln's grades were never very good, though tests showed him to be very intelligent; but his grades absolutely plummeted when he entered junior high school, following the break from his father. He couldn't concentrate on the subjects because of the problems at home, and his appearance made him shy about meeting new people. His report card showed only failing marks at the end of the year, yet he was passed.

In eighth grade Waln was placed in a special education class where he and his classmates were regarded as dummies by mainstream students. Waln's group, in turn, didn't try to fit in. While classes were changing, he and his peers would stand in the halls, greasy hair slicked back, making rude remarks and provoking fights with the other students as they passed by. But the easier work in the special education class allowed Waln to raise his grades to a B average, prompting his transfer into a slightly more challenging curriculum at midyear. His grades fell to just a C+ average but were good enough to promote him to high school freshman. Freshman year, however, proved traumatic for Waln. Circumstances at home had not improved, his complexion had not cleared, and he was inappropriately placed in an advanced academic class. Again his grades fell, and he made no friends as he stumbled over Latin and advanced Algebra. He started to expect rejection and failure while his teachers were also beginning to expect him to create a disturbance in their classes. His detentions started to mount, as did his absences from school. Not surprisingly, Waln failed the freshman year.

The following fall, Waln was placed in a slower paced academic class, more in line with his demonstrated ability. But the fact that others knew he was repeating the grade made him feel more self-conscious and recalcitrant. Convinced he wouldn't get friends, respect, or recognition for anything he did, he began fighting and disrupting classes to get attention. One of the few times he felt respected by his classmates, he recalls, was after he had trounced the class bully, who had started a fight with him. His behavior became more uncontrollable as he started spending time with a group of other boys who never seemed to do anything right either. His class attendance steadily decreased, while his confinement in detention halls increased dramatically. Waln's reputation as a delinquent began to spread among teachers and classmates, with one incident serving as a clincher.

The incident occurred during an art class, when Waln and a friend were disciplined by a teacher for disrupting the class. The teacher finally threatened to hit Waln's friend if he didn't calm down. Unbeknownst to the teacher, Waln pulled out a knife that he handed to his friend under the table. Many of the students saw the weapon, although it was never used. Waln's image as a tough guy spread throughout the school, and he did nothing to discourage it. He even actively encouraged it by ordering people around and playing on their fears.

Although Waln effectively alienated himself from most of the student body at school, he did make some friends over the years. He describes the gang of boys he befriended as misfits. Since Waln and his friends didn't seem to belong anywhere, they decided they belonged together. Each of the six boys in the gang had problems at home and different reasons why he didn't want to spend time there. Together they built motorized bicycles which they used to terrorize the neighborhood. A cigar store became the favorite hangout where the boys would pool their money and play pinball until their pockets were empty. Fashioning switchblade knives, they frightened away larger boys who picked on them. They also started spending time with a gang of older youths who liked to fight and drag race. Waln and his friends tried to emulate the gang members' every move. He spent more time with his friends as he felt tensions build at home. Before long, he and Jack, commonly thought to be the leader of the group, decided to run away, thinking Florida would be a good destination. They left one day after school and followed the railroad tracks through the night. Finally stopping for food at a diner, the boys overheard two police officers discussing a pair of runaway boys. Turning quickly, without finishing their food, Waln and Jack retraced their steps back home.

Back at school, Waln learned that being a bully had its obligations. One day, sitting alone during lunch, he was approached
by another student who wanted to know just how tough Waln
was. Waln tried to ignore the boy, but the challenger punched
him in the face. Grabbing the boy's neck, Waln retaliated by
repeatedly beating his attacker's head into a door. Other students finally pulled them apart. The fight was the last straw for
the school. Waln was suspended, and a juvenile probation officer was called into his case. Because he was still under 15 and
legally required to attend school, he was placed in the county
detention center where classes were held. Now, he felt unwanted not only by his family, but by the school as well. Certainly he was "no good," he thought.

Waln's room at the detention center was a chicken-wire cage
with a cot and a locker. During any free time and at night, he
and the other boys at the detention center were locked in. In
the ten days he spent at the detention center, Waln heard numerous stories from the other boys. Many of their tales paralleled
his own, with family problems often behind the confused and
hurt faces telling the story. Arguments and fights broke out
almost constantly at the detention center; even classrooms were
just another place to cause disruptions.

On the eleventh day a probation officer escorted Waln to court
where his fate was to be decided. He was charged with skipping
school and with the earlier aborted attempt to run away from
home. The judge officially labeled Waln "delinquent" but did
not send him to a school for delinquent boys. Instead, the judge
ordered him released to his mother's custody, where he would
live under probation and attend school. He was also ordered to
return to the court after the school year finished so that his
progress might be assessed. He was to be monitored by his
probation officer. After years of thinking he was "no good,"
now Waln had what he regarded as official proof in the form of
adjudication. After all, he thought, probation officers are given
to criminals. He felt as if everyone were waiting for him to make
his next mistake.

Two months after the court hearing, with his probation officer
recording Waln's every move, with psychologists and psychia-
trists trying to understand his problems, and with his mother

and grandparents not knowing what to do, Waln was given a new wonder drug to help his acne. The acne didn't clear up, but Waln started to feel drugged, as if he were on a hallucinogenic trip most of the time. One day, soon after he started the medication, Waln screamed that he was going to cut his face with a razor and that he hoped a car would hit him as he ran from his house. As night fell, Waln made his way back to his house where he huddled in a corner of the back porch until his mother found him there and called the police.

Waln was taken to the hospital where he awoke to his mother holding his hand. Although she told him she loved him, he didn't believe her and told her she was just like "him"—Waln's father—and that he knew she never loved him. He became so upset that he became violent, throwing a pitcher and kicking at nurses. He was sedated and taken to a padded cell where for three days he fought off all approaches by hospital staff by throwing his body and any furniture he could find at the door. He repeatedly threatened to kill anyone who dared enter. Finally, too weak to fight, he collapsed. He again awoke to find his head in his mother's lap. Sobbing and pleading, he asked her to take him away and promised that he would be good. In the end, however, he was sent to the Harrisburg State Hospital—a mental institution.

His mother described it as a place where he could "get better." What Waln found was a building that smelled of stale urine and feces. His clothes were replaced with a hospital gown, and he was placed in a room with several older men, most of whom lived in their own worlds. No one told Waln that he was to be in the hospital for as many as 90 days so he could be diagnosed. Because he now questioned his own sanity, he believed he was there for infinity. He was prescribed drugs that made him drowsy and soon learned how to hide them in his mouth to avoid swallowing. Doctors came and questioned him but showed no signs of caring, so Waln's responses were always guarded, without going into any depth about his real problems. Visits from his family did no good: his mother often left in tears and Waln refused to speak with his grandmother at all.

He made brief friendships with two patients who were close to his age, but they soon left the hospital. Younger staff members—candy stripers and college interns—also offered him conversation, cigarettes, and a casual friendship, which Waln greedily accepted. But most of Waln's time in the hospital was spent walking alone, marking time. He began to withdraw deeper and deeper into himself to avoid the confusion around him. Waln remained in the hospital for two and a half months, undergoing psychiatric assessment. Doctors finally determined Waln to be highly intelligent, but with poor social and personal adjustment. He also showed early signs of a more severe psychological disorder. Many of the doctors held little hope for his full recovery, but they approved his parole to his mother's care.

At first, the return home was idyllic. Waln was greeted with hugs and kisses, his favorite meals, and a general sense of family togetherness. But soon the old routine of people yelling—mostly at him—returned. The tenth grade went no better than the ninth. Waln was accepted into an industrial/vocational learning program so he could learn a trade. Half of his time was spent on academic work and the other half on industrial projects. Waln began to fail both. His skin became even more inflamed with acne, and other students often made fun of his appearance, leading to more fights.

Waln turned 16 in October of his sophomore year, but his mother and probation officer would not let him quit school because they thought he needed an education. He himself believed he would be better off getting a job to help his mother with bills so that perhaps they could afford an apartment on their own, but he was overruled. His attendance at school fell off to only a few days a week. Every morning began with Waln and his mother arguing over his trumped-up excuse for not attending school that day. But eventually, even he tired of his own excuses, so he simply didn't go to school. He was expelled from one school because of truancy and never showed up for admittance into the next. But the principal soon called Waln's mother, and he returned to school. However, Waln's complete disregard for the school rules soon landed him in enough trouble to warrant calling a juvenile court hearing.

The brief hearing resulted in Waln's placement in the Pennsylvania Junior Republic, a home for delinquent boys. He was sentenced to the Republic for an indefinite period, his release being contingent on administrators deciding he was reformed enough to face the world. On a snowy January day in 1961, a handcuffed Waln was driven to the reform school that housed nearly 350 boys in seven cottages. Other buildings on the campus included classrooms, administration, chapel, swimming pool, and gymnasium. Waln was assigned a cottage and given clothing, and then marched to his cottage where the house parent, "Uncle John," ordered another boy to find a locker for Waln and then left the room.

The trials and hazing began immediately. Some boys started asking for or taking cigarettes from Waln, while others asked or demanded favors of him to do their chores and laundry. In the midst of this chaos, two boys parted the crowd and came up to sort through Waln's possessions. They took whatever they thought looked good and then sauntered away. The rest of the crowd around Waln dispersed since all the good things were already taken. He slept little his first night at PJR. When he did manage to drift off, his dreams were filled with horror; he'd tossed and turned so violently that he awoke to find his sheets tangled and hanging from the side of his bed.

Slowly he was taught the PJR routine, which included shining floors, lining up for meals, and other group assignments and individual chores. He learned to march in step and snap to attention on command. On Saturdays he could watch a movie; on Sundays he went to church; and during the week he marched around the school grounds performing whatever chores were assigned. After twenty-eight days of orientation in the cottage with Uncle John, Waln was moved to a new building and expected to become a regular, school-attending "citizen" of PJR.

Initiation into the new cottage went much the same as his first day. As soon as the house parent left, the other boys surrounded Waln and began making their demands. He was better prepared to handle the situation this time. When one boy came up demanding cigarettes, Waln held his ground and stared into the boy's eyes until the boy turned away. There would be many more trials, but he had won this one. Waln soon learned the new routine that went along with the move to the new cottage. Among the biggest changes was his admission to the PJR school where he was placed in tenth grade. His classes at the reform school were easier, and the teachers were usually big men who didn't stand for any disruptions in their classes. Waln was also given plenty of time to work on his assignments, so he began to do well in all his subjects.

School work wasn't all that Waln learned. He soon became aware of the elaborate social structure or pecking order in place at PJR. It affected everyone and governed how responsibilities and rewards were distributed. The staff and administrator were structured like a family: the PJR director, known as the father, was called "Pappy," and the house parents were known as aunts and uncles. Among the "citizens," as the boys were called, there was a definite order. Some citizens were given special privileges and rewards because they were judged by the administration to demonstrate leadership qualities in socially appropriate ways. If a citizen maintained good grades, he was given the option of going to school in town. This privilege meant going to a regular school, with girls. The president of the student council was the highest ranking citizen. He had power to change things at PJR because he made known to administration the needs of the rest of the student body. The other citizens showed respect for his authority. Next to the president were the individual cottage representatives to the student council, who communicated the group needs to the president of the student council. Night watchman was another coveted position because this person had the run of the school while the adults were asleep. He was responsible for reporting emergencies and looking for runaways.

There was even a hierarchy within each cottage. The floorwalker was the boy who kept watch during the night so there would be no trouble in the cottage. Since the floorwalker reported any problems to the adults, he held great power. The head kitchen boy was next because he was able to tell people what to do and was in charge of six or seven kitchen boys. The laundry boy was next on the hierarchy, but his only real privilege was to be allowed into the laundry where only the floorwalker was otherwise allowed. Jobs filtered down in privileges and responsibility from here.

Unofficially, there were high-ranking members of cottages known as "wheels." These were the fighters whom everyone feared. Wheels got plenty of food and the best locker positions.

Lowest in the order were the "suckies," who informed on other members of the cottage; then came the "flunkies," usually frail boys who did favors in return for protection from the wheels; finally, came the "scurfs," who usually had poor hygiene and were treated like the plague or as objects in sex play by the rest of the citizens. Fights were a daily occurrence and served two purposes: they vented frustrations, and winners were given some respect for their abilities. It was under this order that the citizens functioned and learned to live.

At PJR, every boy was given a job when he entered and then could move up the ladder from there. Waln was given the position of the chaplain's assistant. He asked for the position because he thought it would appeal to his grandmother and other family members who thought the religious life was a good life. The job also gave him plenty of time to do homework and write letters. He spent much of his time writing letters to his mother, letters full of what he thought his problems were and how he wanted to work to change them. They would close with his telling his mother how much he loved her. Waln admits he was very manipulative and tried as many angles as he could think of to gain his release. Since his sentence was for an indefinite amount of time, he knew the administration would release him only when they thought he was ready to face the outside world and he had actually changed. Waln figured that conforming behavior was one way to show he was ready for release. Not everything Waln did was consciously manipulative, however.

Changes began to occur within Waln as he slowly took control of his life. Although punishment at PJR was harsh for boys who broke the rules, Waln says the factor that helped him most to change was gaining recognition and rewards for his good behavior. Before PJR, he had gained what little respect he felt in school from fighting, and thus displaying physical superiority over another person, and at home, he received attention when he caused a disturbance or got in trouble. The first improvement he noticed was in his physical appearance. Through a strict diet, cleansing, and medicating regime prescribed by the dermatologist at PJR, the acne that had made Waln so ashamed and self-conscious started to disappear. Another physical change was Waln's normal growth, which made him a 6-foot, 170-pound young man. His physical prowess earned him quite a reputation among his peers. With this new bit of self-confidence he started applying himself to his school work even more. He decided to prove he wasn't stupid. With good grades, he would be placed on the honor roll and earn weekend passes to home. Furthermore, he thought that such diligence would aid in his quest to be released. Instead of detention slips, Waln started to receive compliments from teachers for his good work. Other students started to look up to him as a good scholastic example. At the end of tenth grade, he was chosen as an outstanding student, the first time he truly felt proud of himself.

Waln took summer school classes as well so that he could advance to the eleventh grade on time. His good grades and behavior would have allowed him to attend regular school in town, but Waln wisely decided he wasn't ready to leave the safe haven of the PJR school just yet. He also started playing team sports and found he excelled, becoming captain of several of the teams on which he played. Waln started advancing through the ranks in his cottage as well. He was named temporary floorwalker and eventually became the full-time floorwalker.

Before long, Waln was even named student council representative from his cottage. While his self-respect grew, he remained suspicious of adults and was still a bully. Desperately wanting praise and release, he often pointed out his good deeds in letters to his family and his probation officer, and fished for compliments from the administration. Waln asked to leave more than one job at PJR when his good deeds went unnoticed. After eighteen months at PJR, he was released. The administration acknowledged that, although Waln was still physically aggressive and could be manipulative in trying to get what he wanted, he seemed ready to face the outside world.

Waln had some difficulties in adjustment when he returned home. The old problems and tensions resulting from his mother's and his grandparents' failing health still pervaded the small household. In addition, he had to face a somewhat unstructured life again. For nearly two years Waln had been institutionalized and given directions and strict guidelines to follow. He still had to account to his probation officer, but there was no constant supervision. Waln left the Pennsylvania Juvenile Republic in

1962, and, although he hadn't completely changed the behaviors that resulted in his placement there, he never became an adult criminal.

Waln's experience at the institution, his budding self-esteem, and his growing maturity helped him deal with most problems as they arose. He also had strong desire not to be institutionalized again. Knowing that if he started spending time with his old friends, he would be headed for trouble, he made new friends, and his looks and attitude improved. His greased hair and tough guy clothes and actions gave way to a more Ivy League appearance. He got a job that allowed him to contribute money to the family as he desired to do, and still have money left to buy clothing to help him maintain his improved look. The summer passed with few problems. However, going back to a school from which he had been previously expelled offered more of a challenge. Waln's classmates were generally wealthier than he, and his reputation as a "tough guy," fighter, and reform school graduate circulated quickly. The course work was also harder than he had encountered at PJR, and by the end of the year, Waln's grades were barely sufficient to graduate; but he did. At first, he thought graduation was the answer to all of his problems; he was a free man without school work to hold him back.

But life in the real world wasn't as easy as Waln had anticipated. After losing his first job, he tried to join the military but was rejected for psychological reasons. His feelings of inadequacy and being unwanted started to surface again as he lost many jobs during the next two years. The reasons varied but ultimately involved something Waln did or did not do. To make matters worse, his family sorely needed his income. As when he was 13, his family was depending on him, and he did not feel up to the responsibility. Because both grandparents died within two years of each other, their social security benefits were no longer available to the family. Furthermore, since Waln had reached 18, child support payments had ceased. Waln started frequenting bars where the evening often ended in a fist fight. Looking back, he says he fought until he was 21. He doesn't remember how the change occurred after that age, but he does recall walking into a bar with a friend and saying he didn't want to hurt anyone any more, and then feeling good to be in charge of that part of his life. But as his twenty-first birthday approached, he was still without direction. He finally applied to York Junior College in hopes that he could learn a trade or become a teacher in four years. His mother agreed that she could handle the family finances as long as Waln could pay his school bills, so he secured financial aid and headed for college.

Although he did poorly his first year, ending with a grade point average of 1.4, Waln was determined to return in autumn to do better. But during the summer he worked for a furniture company and was offered a job as a salesman. He also met a girl, Sally, and fell in love. When school started again, Waln did not return. He no longer dreamed of completing college but of making enough money to marry Sally. Unfortunately, within the year, he left the furniture store, which had turned out to be a dead end, and he lost Sally. She had gone away to college, deciding that Waln was too uneducated and "dull" for her. He was devastated for months because losing Sally reopened many old and festering wounds of past rejections. He lost weight and was sometimes suicidal. Then one day his best friend, a college student, asked Waln how long he was going to waste his life, and told him to read Voltaire's *Candide*. Out of respect for his friend, Waln read *Candide*. He was fascinated by the book and soon wanted to know more. He devoured as many books as he could find. Five years after his release from reform school, Waln's life took a definite positive direction. He moved to the west coast and started taking college courses there.

Life showed more promise with every success. A letter from Sally rekindled Waln's hopes of marriage and a blissful life, but she soon called to say she was engaged to another. This time, he didn't take this blow as life threatening; he was too full of desire for a college education. Returning to Pennsylvania, he worked full time at an air freight company and again entered York Junior College. Waln graduated with a 2.14 grade point average and an associate degree in liberal studies. Buoyed by a new sense of accomplishment, he entered Pennsylvania State University and earned a baccalaureate degree in less than two years by taking extra courses and attending summer school. The following summer he began graduate courses at the University of Pennsylvania, where he eventually earned not only a master of arts, but a Ph.D.! His doctoral dissertation dealt with understanding the subculture of gangs and what it provided for young inner-city Blacks. He was fascinated by the subject, but dismayed to find that the literature portrayed such grim prospects for delinquent youth. Thus, Waln began to look into his own life to try to find why he was now living a relatively normal adult life after such a trouble-fraught youth. He is still studying delinquent youth and working to find positive outcomes in hopes of creating more successes.

Reflecting on his life, Waln says his life might have been different if his parents had stayed married, or if his father had taken an active role in his son's life. Waln would probably not have felt such devastating guilt and abandonment from his parents' breakup, nor felt such helpless vulnerability in the face of the debility of the adults in his life. Institutionalization in the Pennsylvania Junior Republic was perhaps the most significant element in his turnaround. It took him out of a very troubled household and provided a respite for the struggling adults who didn't know what to do with him or for him. By providing the highly structured environment that he desperately needed, PJR taught him how to excel and gain recognition without resorting to disruptive measures. The timing of Waln's release from PJR was also important. Going back to regular school was too much for Waln to manage well; if he'd had more than one year to graduation, he most likely would have failed, possibly resulting in continued delinquent activity, reflecting his very poor self-esteem. Waln sees structure, consistent discipline, achievement, and recognition as critical to positive outcomes for troubled youth. He also says it is extremely important to look for the good in children, because emphasizing the bad can lead only to alienation and failure.

A SEARCH FOR SIGNIFICANT FACTORS

While not married, for the past five years, Waln has had an exclusive live-in relationship with the mother of two children whom he has accepted as his own. "They are my family," he states. All indications are that he has developed into a productive and sensitive adult who is not emotionally handicapped by the low self-esteem, sense of rejection, and institutionalization that characterized his turbulent childhood and adolescent years. While certainly not definitive, the research literature generally supports a negative outcome for children of extensive parental discord, rejection, and divorce. Although psychological and psychiatric evaluations uniformly offered a poor prognosis for Waln, he succeeded despite the odds. What factors appear important in his triumph? The following suggests some clues.

Mother's Relationship

Waln's mother was described as being overprotective primarily because of his early bouts with rheumatic fever and anemia. While her actions may have strengthened her relationship with him, it was a source of parental discord and created a strain between Waln and his father. Although the mother's overly protective behavior may have been a result of her own emotional instability, it is mentioned as a potential significant factor in Waln's development because he apparently found consolation in the relationship and used it as protection from what he perceived as a hostile and rejecting world. Even though his relationship with his mother was threatened and was never as close, according to Waln, as a result of his first institutionalization, he yearned to regain the closeness. In the midst of his intense emotional reaction to his perceived parental rejection, he strove to retain his mother's positive regard.

Institutionalization

Although he did not consider it at the time, Waln now unequivocally believes that being institutionalized was his "saving grace." According to Waln, placement at PJR came at a time when he so desperately needed "direction, structure, and strict guidelines" in his life. His acne cleared up while at PJR, resulting in reduced anxiety about his appearance and increased self-concept. At least as significant, for the first time in his life, Waln felt he received recognition and rewards for engaging in socially appropriate behavior. The parental discord and ultimate separation between his father and mother probably precluded them from dispensing social approval in a systematic manner. His intense emotional reaction to his familial problems could have predisposed him to aggressive acting-out behavior, thus making him more receptive to recognition for engaging in his early socially inappropriate behavior. PJR provided Waln the environment in which he could detach himself from his familial problems and concentrate on improving his own self-esteem. At PJR, Waln consciously sought to receive approval for his good deeds; when these deeds went unnoticed in one activity, he would quickly move to another where they would be noticed. While initially he was apparently manipulative in engaging in socially appropriate behaviors to receive rewards and praise, he ultimately internalized the desire and became genuine in his efforts to gain approval through such behaviors.

According to Waln, the timing of his release from PJR was also significant; he only had to complete the twelfth grade once he returned to public school. While institutionalization provided Waln with increased self-esteem and a sense of accomplishment, being released with more than a year left in school would have eroded the gains he had made. He felt that returning to public school was very stressful in itself, and when coupled with continued familial problems, Waln has the impression that he would not have been able to cope with the mounting pressure.

Personality Factors

Interview data indicated that Waln had a strong desire not to be institutionalized. Something about Waln's personality prevented him from becoming a juvenile who favored living in rather than outside of an institution. This orientation caused him to seek out ways of pleasing others as a means of being released. Once released from PJR, Waln's fear of re-institutionalization caused him to abandon his old friends and to gain new ones. His conscious decision to develop new friends required a tremendous amount of insight and was one that few adolescents can make and maintain. He obviously possessed the intellectual and social ability to excel academically and socially, and once some of the emotional pain associated with his familial problems was removed, these abilities manifested themselves.

Objective personality assessment indicates that Waln's personality orientation is introverted; he is somewhat shy and can be quite jealous, overprotective, and suspicious. Waln is extremely sensitive. Contrary to his earlier orientation, he prefers to use logic rather than force to achieve desired goals. Consistent with his introverted lifestyle, Waln prefers to work alone; however, when working in groups he would rather lead. In addition, he has strict moral standards and generally conforms to acceptable levels of standards. He is conscientious, being strongly oriented toward fulfilling his obligations. Having a tendency to feel more anxious than most people, he may be perceived as an emotionally tense and driven individual.

Despite the extreme pain and suffering of his youth, all indications are that Waln has successfully adjusted. He has succeeded personally, socially, and professionally. He has a positive orientation toward life and is dedicating a significant amount of his time to understanding his own problems in hopes of helping other youth who may experience similar problems. While a uniquely personal story, his life offers much insight into a youth who experienced parental divorce and the associated feelings of rejection, hostility, and emotional liability.

CHAPTER FIVE

Succeeding Despite a Learning Disability

Most people, lay and professional alike, have heard the term *learning disability*, but when pressed to clarify the term, they offer widely varying definitions. The definitions have ranged from "minimally brain damaged" and "mildly retarded" to "emotionally disturbed." This confusion is understandable because experts in the field do not themselves agree on the definition of learning disability. Nor is there universal consensus as to the specific factors that cause it. It is certain that some individuals, for a variety of reasons, have severe problems in learning. Such problems at the very least, result in anxiety, frustration, and dissatisfaction with the formal learning process. Learning disabled children may have difficulty in auditory and/or visual perception, may have a significant delay in speech acquisition, may misunderstand the spoken word, may hear clearly but be unable to accurately process what is heard, and so on. These children may look and talk normally and show competencies in many different areas; some have above-average intelligence but demonstrate extreme difficulties in the language arts, including reading and/or writing. Some show severe problems in mathematics. Such learning problems are usually first recognized and diagnosed when the child is confronted with the learning tasks required in school.

The most widely accepted definition of learning disabilities is included in the Education for All Handicapped Children Act (1975) and is contained in Public Law 94–142 enacted in 1977:

"Specific learning disability" means a disorder in one or more of the basic psychological processes involved in understanding or in using language, spoken or written, which may manifest itself in an imperfect ability to listen, think, speak, read, write, spell, or to do mathematical calculations. The term includes such conditions as perceptual handicaps, brain injury, minimal brain dysfunction, dyslexia, and developmental aphasia. The term does not include children who have learning problems which are primarily the result of visual, hearing, or motor handicaps, of mental retardation, of emotional disturbance, or of environmental, cultural, or economic disadvantage. (Lerner, 1988, p. 7)

While this federal definition is widely accepted, much criticism still abounds, attesting to the lack of consensus in defining the disorder (Feagans, 1983). However, several basic points relative to defining learning disability can be highlighted, some of which come from the federal definition described above and others which are widely accepted in the literature. First, the term *learning disability* represents a heterogeneous class of disabilities; for example, the learning disabled individual may have a deficit in any or all of the basic psychological processes. Second, a learning disability results in the individual's having problems in learning, not primarily caused by other conditions, such as hearing or visual loss, or mental retardation. Third, the cause of the learning disability is within the individual and not the environment. Social, economic, and educational factors may intensify the problems experienced by the learning disabled child, but they are secondary and not causative. Fourth, the learning disability causes a severe discrepancy between an individual's potential and his or her level of achievement. As suggested earlier, professionals do not agree on the definition of learning disability. Therefore, the four basic points described should not be considered all inclusive. These basic points represent the major themes that experts in the field often mention when defining the term.

The prevalence of learning disability in the school population ranges from 1 to 30 percent, depending on the definition used (Lerner, 1988). It is estimated that over 2 million students are affected by various forms of learning disability. The number of children believed to have a learning disability is larger than any other group of handicapped students, including the mentally retarded, emotionally disturbed, and speech and hearing impaired (Myers and Hammill, 1990). Boys more often than girls are diagnosed as learning disabled. Dyslexia, an inability to read or extreme problems in learning to read, is the most common form of learning disability.

Just because a child has learning problems does not mean the child is learning disabled. The term *learning disability* is used to describe a particular class of individuals who have problems in learning. Furthermore, despite its typical use to describe learning problems in school, learning disability is not a condition restricted to childhood. One may receive treatment for the disability or simply learn to adjust to it, but there is no known cure. Several well-known historical figures were learning disabled and became successful despite it. Thomas Edison, the American inventor, and Albert Einstein, the mathematician, are said to have been learning disabled. Nelson Rockefeller, former vice-president of the United States and governor of the state of New York, described his feelings about growing up with a learning disability:

I was dyslexic . . . and I still have a hard time reading today. I remember vividly the pain and mortification I felt as a boy of eight when I was assigned to read a short passage of scripture at a community vesper service and did a thoroughly miserable job of it. I know what a dyslexic child goes through . . . the frustration of not being able to do what other children do easily, the humiliation of being thought not too bright when such is not the case at all. But after coping with this problem for more than 60 years, I have a message of hope and encouragement for children with learning disabilities—and their parents. (Lerner, 1988, p. 4)

While Rockefeller was able to overcome his learning disability and become successful, many learning disabled children do not. Many such children manifest social/emotional or behavioral problems as a result of their inability to learn normally. Feagan states:

Thus a learning disability, although considered a mild handicap, continues to affect the child throughout the school years. Unfortunately, many professionals and parents often minimize the long-term academic and social consequences because of the other perceived competencies of these children. Studies of learning-disabled adolescents indicate that the increasing demands at the secondary level actually produce more numerous and more varied difficulties, including academic, social, and emotional problems. (p. 489)

Unable to perform adequately in school, these children may turn their frustration outward, leading to acting out behaviors, such as fighting and delinquency. Alternatively, they may turn the frustration inward, resulting in feelings of depression, learned helplessness, poor self-esteem, and the like. What factors contribute to an individual's overcoming his or her learning disability?, is the question asked by the following case study. The answer to this question may provide valuable insight for those suffering from a learning disability.

THE CASE OF KAE

In 1985 at the age of 36, Kae was formally diagnosed as learning disabled. By that time, she already held her doctorate in education and was the principal of an elementary school. No one had told her she wasn't supposed to be able to do that. "People have the misconception that a learning disability means a lack of intelligence," she said during an interview in her school office while new age music floated through the air.

Kae says she was in second grade when she realized she wasn't understanding things as everyone else was. All her school friends were reading with fluidity while she was struggling with each word. She never thought to ask the other children if letters floated and moved on their pages as they did on hers. She thought everyone else must have learned some code that she couldn't figure out. Kae was always the last student to finish class assignments and usually had to take unfinished class work home for homework. As a result, she didn't like school.

One day Kae's second grade teacher told the class that anyone who didn't finish his or her class work would have to stay in the classroom until it was completed. A police officer would patrol the area at night to make sure the student was not hurt, the teacher declared. Kae was terrified. She knew that no matter how hard she worked, she would never finish her work on time; she decided that once she got out of the school that day, she would never come back. Of course, her parents made her go back to school and even accompanied Kae there when she explained her fear. The teacher said she had been joking about keeping the students, but Kae remained wary of the school system for many years after that.

In third grade, Kae still was not reading and was placed with the slower students in her class. At the end of the year, when she had not shown much improvement, the school began to deliberate over whether she should be held back a year. Kae's parents convinced the school to let her be promoted to fourth grade. She spent this school year at the dining room table with her father who tried desperately to get her to understand reading letter sounds in combinations to make words, and math problems with words in them.

Kae's saving grace was her parents. Learning disabilities were not clearly recognized or understood in the 1950s when Kae was growing up. Her parents spent many hours frustrated with what seemed their daughter's inability to learn, but they never showed their frustration to their daughter. Kae felt that she was stupid because she was having so many problems in school, but that was not the message she received at home.

Kae's father, a self-taught mechanical engineer, was especially helpful to her. He spent many hours during her school years trying to help her with her homework whenever he could. He also came up with many different creative ways to keep her interested and working. He was the role model and character builder in the family. Kae attributes her adherence to the work ethic today to her father's teachings. Her father was the first person to see the spark of intelligence in Kae. When she was little, she always asked why she had to do something. Her father soon realized that her questions were not idle and that she really wanted and needed to know the reasoning behind requests her parents made. For example, she wouldn't sit down in the car until the accident risks were explained to her.

Kae's parents were also very careful never to compare her to her older brother, who graduated second in his class and never had any problems learning. At the beginning of each school year, Kae's parents instructed her teachers that Kae was not her brother and that no comparisons should be made between the two children.

Kae says she knew her brother was better in school than she was, but through her parents' attitude about the two children she rarely felt jealousy or rivalry toward her sibling. She was assured by her parents that she was not inferior. They forcefully insisted that she attend school regularly and would accept no excuses or faked illnesses. Her parents were tough, but fair and helpful to Kae whenever they could be.

Kae's parents never doubted her intelligence but didn't understand her reading and organizational problems. They honestly and wholeheartedly answered, "No!" when Kae asked if she were mentally retarded.

Her grades stayed in the C range, which Kae's grandmother declared was because Kae wasn't trying. But Kae's parents knew their daughter was giving the work her all and praised her for her effort rather than her grades. They also looked beyond the schools to help her. In the sixth grade, where Kae describes her learning as trial and error, her parents saw an advertisement for a set of records that guaranteed to increase a child's reading ability. They bought the set and assigned Kae the task of sitting and listening to them for hours. Kae's window overlooked an empty field where she loved to play. She would look out at the field as the record repeated words and instructions again and again. The field beckoned her. Being a wily and intelligent young girl, Kae devised a plan. She timed the record. Once she turned the droning on, she would climb out her window to play, returning only to turn the record over. Her plan worked two or three times until one afternoon, when Kae crawled in her window to find her mother waiting for her. Kae's mother kept her company during the record sessions after that.

As she moved into seventh grade, Kae developed another system, similar to the one used with the records, to get out of reading. The actions she took are called "coping skills" today, but were nameless at the time Kae began using them. Like many learning disabled children, Kae realized that her listening comprehension and memory skills were very good. If she listened to a person read or describe a book, she could remember it. In the seventh grade, Kae moved toward the front of the class so she could hear better. She was still reading on a second or third grade level, but listening helped her complete her class work and answer more questions on tests. She still had trouble finishing the tests because they involved reading, but what work she could complete was usually correct.

Kae's school vacations were spent in reading clinics and summer schools. In the summer of her tenth grade year, Kae's father paid $600 for Kae to attend a special college preparatory clinic at the local university. After weeks of reading instruction, the instructors told Kae's father that all Kae needed to do to succeed in school was to read more. The next summer, Kae's father saved most of the $600 and spent money on magazine subscriptions which Kae had to promise to read.

Parents tend to become angry when they have learning disabled children, Kae said. The parents want the schools to fix the problems, but the best schools have done is try to teach the children to cope. In Kae's case, the schools weren't sure what would help her cope. But Kae was rapidly developing her own skills to pass. She set her goals on what she needed to do to get out of the school system she so disliked so that she could have her own life. At the same time, she made sure she was keeping her grades high enough to stay in all the extracurricular activities in which she took part.

During her entire school career, Kae continuously got in trouble for talking during class and missed many recesses because of it—that is, when she wasn't already staying in to finish her school work. Kae says it was her frustration with the work which led her to talk so much. She disliked the work because it was so hard, and she sought a diversion from it.

As Kae got older she started getting involved in clubs. A small, perky, cheerful young woman, she became president of her school's pep club, the junior class president, yearbook editor, a band member, and was voted class clown by her classmates. Her friendly personality became her greatest asset in her studies.

In high school Kae chose her friends carefully. She looked for patient people who wouldn't mind reteaching her again and again what the teacher had tried to do with one lesson. She and her friends got together to work on homework in a group. They read the questions, and Kae helped with the answers. Once the problems were completed, Kae copied the finished product on her own paper. She figured it wasn't really cheating because she had been involved in working out the original answer.

Kae finally managed to finish high school. Although she didn't graduate with distinction, she graduated. She started working for the Easter Seals Foundation and as a waitress. Part of Kae's job with Easter Seals was to help teach small children with handicaps. She did such a good job that she was encouraged to think about going to college. Her parents had always told her that they would support her if she wanted to go. Kae decided to go to college, but not because she wanted to fulfill any burning desire to work with handicapped children. She decided to go because she found working as a waitress very hard, and she figured reading would be easier than being a waitress for the rest of her life.

Kae chose her college using the same determined precision with which she chose her friends. The school would have to be small so she could receive individual attention and extra help if she needed it. She was also a very religious young woman and wanted to be in a religiously affiliated school. Kae chose a small Methodist affiliated college in North Carolina. Kae's first major was sociology. However, her studies in that area lasted only about three weeks, because she learned she would have to study a foreign language to graduate. After her great difficulty with Latin in high school, the last thing she wanted to tackle was another foreign language. She majored in religion for about a year before finally deciding that being an elementary school teacher might not be such a bad idea.

Kae began to form symbiotic relationships with the other students in her major. She would help them with their algebra if they would help her with her reading. She bought used books with passages already underlined and took advantage of the student underground to find out the different teaching styles of various professors. Kae's favorite classes were those in which the professor tested directly from the notes given in classes. She knew that all she had to do in those classes was pay strict attention. She always looked for the easiest angle.

But Kae's attitude toward education changed during her college days. She had always looked on school as an unavoidable hassle and had approached her studies from the perspective, "What do I have to do to get out of here?" But in college Kae discovered that she truly wanted to learn, and she convinced herself that she could do it. One day, Kae visited the office of two English professors, both of whom told Kae that she simply didn't have the reading skills to make it in college. Without a pause Kae asked which of them would be the one to teach her. Both professors took on the responsibility. Also, some of Kae's roommates were English majors. She took three times as long to finish a project as one of her roommates, but then she got them to check what she had done. Her roommates patiently made corrections to Kae's finished work. Kae tutored her classmates in math, and they would make her bulletin boards for her education classes. By maximizing her adaptation skills in ways like these, Kae managed to graduate from college in just four years—a pretty remarkable achievement for a learning disabled student.

Kae began teaching and found that she could be a big help to students who had learning problems similar to hers. She easily spotted their tell-tale behavior patterns because they so closely resembled her own. Obsessed with understanding why and how people learn, she started working part-time on a master's degree in psychology, mostly to help understand herself. She finished her master's degree in three years, while teaching full time. She then moved into school administration and started working on her doctorate in education. Kae says she got her master's degree to understand how her mind worked, and then she got her doctorate to remind herself that her mind was working. She says she wanted to prove to herself that she was intelligent. Kae's doctorate, which she completed in four years with some editorial help on her dissertation, is a great comfort to her on particularly frustrating days. After making several spelling or reading errors, Kae reminds herself that she isn't stupid—she has her doctorate!

Education isn't the only area in which Kae had problems. One of the symptoms of her learning disability is a certain disorganization. For example, she never carries a purse. She used to carry one but had a habit of leaving it everywhere she stopped. After leaving and retrieving it three times in one day, Kae promised God that, if it was still intact when she got to it the final time, she would never burden Him with her carrying a purse again.

In her job as a principal, Kae uses her coping skills well and counts her blessings in having found a very organized secretary. The secretary keeps a calendar of all of Kae's appointments and makes sure Kae remembers them. If Kae isn't reminded frequently of tasks or engagements, she will almost certainly forget as other thoughts invade her mind.

Understanding people has helped Kae with both her job and her personal life. She is now divorced but was married for five years to a man whom she believes is also learning disabled but was never diagnosed. She describes him as a very bright, sensitive, responsible man. He was also an alcoholic and was honest with her about his problem when they married. Still, Kae says she chose her husband as she had chosen her friends in the past; she wanted a stable home with a husband, and she thinks he wanted an intelligent, stable mother for his young son by his first wife.

Before they got married, he had warned her that his personality changed when he started drinking and that the best thing she could do at that time was to get away from him. When he began drinking again, Kae stayed with him for more than a year, trying to help him work through his problems. They worked together for a while, she says, until she tried to get him to stop drinking altogether. Seeing his wife as a barrier to his next drink, he became violent. Eventually, Kae was compelled to take his advice and leave him. She keeps in touch with her stepson and believes she has helped the boy to understand that his father's problems are no reflection on him.

Kae says she still would like to have a home complete with a husband but has long ago become comfortable with herself. Her learning disability, she asserts, has actually helped her overcome setbacks that would probably devastate many nonlearning disabled people. She can cope better because when she was younger she learned to see problems not as failures but as good tries. Most people develop this kind of coping skill only after reaching adulthood.

Kae also talks to herself when she's reading or planning something, concluding that if she hears it she will remember it. She uses a dictaphone to write letters and notes because her verbal and auditory skills are so much better than her written and organizational skills. Letters that used to take her three hours to write now take about 30 minutes. A learning disabled person learns to use all resources available to his or her advantage. Kae learned in college that when she's tired she must rest from academic tasks because her reading problems only worsen. It's all a matter of learning to recognize one's own strengths and weaknesses.

Kae attributes her job success to her openness about her disability. When she applied for her first principal's job, rather than hide her problems, she was honest about them and the school board saw her merits. Kae also says that her years of assessing people who could assist her with her work have made her a very good judge of character, which has helped her with her different teachers and the 600 students she supervises. Soon after a first meeting she can tell how a teacher will approach teaching and how she, as principal, can work with that teacher to reach the desired goals.

Kae has set a goal for her school to help teachers understand what learning disabled children are going through. She also works with the faculties of local colleges to help professors deal with learning disabled adults at the university level.

Kae is very vocal about learning disabilities, for she firmly believes that the more people know about learning problems, the better off children with these problems will be. It is her conviction that for both the teachers and the learning disabled education breeds education: the longer you can keep a learning disabled person working in school, the more that person will want to continue. If the perseverance is there, the student will succeed.

Today, many people who meet Kae don't believe she has a learning disability. That's in part a testimony to her achievements, but it also reflects the common misconception that a person can outgrow a learning disability. Kae explains to as many people as possible that a learning disability is a lifelong handicap. Her friends attest to her writing problems by joking about what a special decoding treat it is to get a handwritten letter from Kae.

Kae thinks growing up in a time before learning disabilities were identified made her life easier. She was placed in a slower group, but she was still in class with the rest of her peers, and she still took college preparatory courses. Unfortunately, American society equates reading with intelligence, so today children with learning disabilities are often placed in special classes apart from their peers. The separation causes many people to equate a learning disability with a lack of intelligence or a retardation. Such, however, is rarely the case. Tests show that Kae's IQ well exceeds 120. (The "average" IQ is about 100.)

Kae says that the learning disabled person is probably his or her own best help. She remembers reading words off a chart with another learning disabled student. They were both reading the same way—with the first letter of the word on the line directly above the word they were reading. The teacher, not understanding what the two were doing, stopped them. Suddenly the words fell correctly for Kae, and she realized what she and the other student were doing. She turned to the other student and explained how he should decipher the sentences to understand the material and answer the teacher's questions. He got the idea and the lesson continued without incident.

With those thoughts in mind, Kae wakes every day and faces her job wondering what she can do to help more kids. She knows it will be difficult for parents, teachers, and the learning disabled students alike, but she wants them all to know the student will learn. They simply have to unlock the code. There is a discrepancy between intelligence and achievement, and some learning disabled people just need to learn that they are not functioning at their full potential.

A SEARCH FOR SIGNIFICANT FACTORS

Kae is a living example of how an individual can overcome tremendous handicaps to succeed. Although Kae and her parents knew that learning was difficult for her, no one expected that she had a learning disability. It was only in her adult years, after having worked extremely hard to succeed academically, that she was ultimately diagnosed as learning disabled. Placing a label on her problem gave her an understanding of why academic tasks were so hard for her. However, it does not tell how Kae was able to excel despite the disability. The factors that contributed to her success is the question still unanswered and the focus of the current inquiry. Some hints of significant factors can be gleaned from Kae's life story.

Parental Influence

Kae attributes much of her success to her parents, whom she fondly calls "My saving grace." Obviously her parents played a very active role in her learning. Her father not only spent time helping her to study and to understand school work but also expended considerable amounts of money to help her to do well in school.

While Kae's parents knew that acquiring academic knowledge was difficult for her, they appeared to have an underlying belief that she was capable of excelling, though at her own pace. As noted earlier, her parents praised her for her efforts and not for her grades. While it was undoubtedly frustrating for Kae's parents to labor so intensely to help their daughter learn what came so easily for their son, Kae does not recall her parents ever demonstrating that frustration to her. Her parents never compared her to her brother, who obviously had no trouble with school work. Her parents also insisted that Kae's teachers not make comparisons.

Kae's parents also seemed to convey the attitude to Kae that she could succeed academically if provided the right resources, which probably gave Kae her perseverance. Her parents paid for tutors, home reading and learning aids, and academic enhancement programs. They even promised to pay for college if Kae chose to attend. It was their belief in her ability that helped her believe in herself, causing her to work hard and not give up, and, most importantly, to look for resources that would help her succeed. Her parents' reliance on resources manifested itself in Kae's life as she carefully chose friends, reading material, study groups, and the like, which would help her do well in school. Without the expectation of success provided by her parents, it is doubtful that Kae would have searched for these resources.

Personality Factors

Kae describes herself as being extremely inquisitive at a very early age. She was considered especially friendly, having a cheerful and positive attitude. Kae was voted class clown by classmates. Undoubtedly, these characteristics put Kae in good favor with friends, making it easy for her to rely on them for help with school work.

Generally, results of personality testing support the observations gathered during the interview. Kae appears secure and extremely self-assured. Despite having a learning disability, her ego-strength appears undamaged, suggesting that her handicap has not negatively affected her personality. She is characterized as having an inquiring mind, being emotionally stable, approaching problems in a calm, realistic manner, and being unpretentious and somewhat naive and venturesome. Overall, she appears to be a confident, genuine, social-minded individual who exercises self-discipline and emotional maturity. Although these characteristics may have been inborn, they were nurtured by Kae's parents during her formative years. In their supportive attitude and behavior regarding her learning problems, her parents provided the foundation for their child's coping skills and achievement-oriented attitude, which was the significant factor leading to Kae's succeeding despite the odds. It would appear that they were indeed her saving grace.

CHAPTER SIX

An Adolescent Parent
Succeeding Despite the Odds

Adolescent pregnancy is a growing concern not only in the United States but throughout the world. Recognizing the international scope of the problem, representatives of some thirty-nine nations met in Virginia in 1976 for the First Interhemispheric Conference on Adolescent Fertility. These representatives debated and suggested changes in social policies, laws, customs, and services to combat the problem. The adolescent pregnancy rate in the United States is one of the highest in the world. "Of 22 selected countries, including both industrialized and under-developed nations, the United States ranks fourth, with a rate of 58 births per 1000 females aged 15–19" (Hendrixson, 1983). This rate is about eight times that in Japan and five times that in Switzerland and the Netherlands (Greene, 1987). According to some estimates, American girls under 15 years of age are at least five times more likely to give birth than same-aged girls in any other developed country.

Numerous complications accompany adolescent pregnancy. For example, babies born to teenage mothers have statistically significant lower birth weight (Walters, 1975). This is a significant factor contributing to the nation's very high infant mortality rate and is particularly true for African Americans (Papalia and Olds, 1992). Surviving low-birth-weight babies may experience a variety of life-threatening conditions, such as immature organ and neurological development, respiratory difficulties, and problems controlling body temperature and blood sugar levels. Babies born to teenagers are more likely to be premature or stillborn and to have birth defects, spinal deformities, or epilepsy. These infants are also more likely to be victims of child abuse and have lower IQ scores (Nye, 1977). Several factors appear to contribute to a poor prognosis for babies born to teenage mothers, including the teenager's own incomplete physical and emotional development, inadequate prenatal care, and poor nutritional habits, as well as poor child-care skills (Hendrixson, 1983).

The adolescent mother also suffers many physical side-effects as a result of her pregnancy. She is more likely to experience birth complications that could result in anemia, toxemia, depression, other diseases, and even death (Alan Guttmacher Institute, 1976). Recent research suggests, however, that the health problems experienced by teenage mothers and their infants are attributable more to social than to medical factors (Brown, 1985). That is, because adolescent mothers tend to be poor, do not eat properly, and receive little or no prenatal care—factors that are socially determined—they are prone to medical complications. The implication, supported by research findings, is that medical complications associated with adolescent pregnancy can be significantly reduced if better nutrition and prenatal care are provided to teenage mothers.

The documented immediate consequences of adolescent pregnancy create a bleak picture for the young girl and her baby. The long-term consequences of adolescent pregnancy don't look any better:

• Poverty and public dependency frequently await the teenage mother and child. (Ferguson, 1990, p. 2)

• Two out of three pregnant teenagers drop out of school. With her education cut short, the teenage mother may lack job skills, which may cause her to live in poverty. The income of teen mothers is half that of those who first gave birth in their twenties. They may be financially dependent on their family or on welfare. (Ferguson, 1990, p. 4)

• Even with the best care and the best of physical outcomes, the fate of teenage parents and their children is often not a happy one. Eighty percent of pregnant teenagers aged 17 and under, and 90 percent of those aged 15 and under, never finish high school. As a result, they often become unemployable and go on welfare, beginning or continuing a cycle of dependency that saps their motivation to achieve success. (Papalia and Olds, 1989, p. 396)

- The discouraging fact is that more than half of the women who receive Aid to Families with Dependent Children were teenagers when they had their first child. (Hulbert, 1984, p. 19)

These findings speak to the poor prognosis for adolescent mothers. Estimates may vary, but they always suggest a high probability of future failure and dysfunction. This negative outcome perspective fuels the desire to prevent adolescent pregnancy and to look for factors that differentiate adolescents who become pregnant from those who do not. Walters, Walters, and McKenry (1987) studied various characteristics known to place adolescents at high risk of becoming pregnant:

Historically, it has been thought that there must be something wrong with young girls who become pregnant. The assumption has not been only their circumstances in life have been different, for we are a nation with a deep belief in the ability of an individual to rise above a deprived environment. The implication has been that young girls who become pregnant are intrinsically different from those who do not. (p. 26)

Understandably, these authors reasoned that if factors could be found which place the adolescent at high risk of becoming pregnant, preventive measures could be instituted (i.e., counseling services, educational programs). Walters, Walters, and McKenry (1987), however, were unsuccessful in identifying the major characteristics that place the adolescent at high risk of pregnancy. According to these authors, we are currently without a comprehensive model that will explain why some young girls become pregnant and others do not. They stated, "Apparently, neither psychological characteristics nor type of family are good predictors of early pregnancy. Thus, it appears that being in the right place at the right time is the precondition to pregnancy" (Walters, Walters, and McKenry, p. 27).

The current chapter is theoretically based on the assumption that high-risk groups can be identified, but a positive outcome focus is stressed. Rhodes has explained this elsewhere:

Instead of looking at why adolescents become pregnant and generating prevention efforts based on the logic obtained (negative outcomes), it may be more useful to look at why these adolescents who were theoretically supposed to become pregnant (high risk) did not become pregnant (positive outcomes). In other words, where did the adolescent go right? (Rhodes and Stevenson, 1991, 79–80)

Stevenson and Rhodes (1991) explored research findings that contribute to answering the question posed above: Where did the adolescent go right? The current chapter asks the same question but with regard to those adolescents who become pregnant. That is, why do some adolescents who become pregnant and keep their babies not experience the multitude of problems characteristically associated with their status—that is, school dropout, welfare dependency, and so on? The authors believe that the prevention of adolescent pregnancy should be vigorously pursued. However, given that some adolescents will become pregnant, we must know and establish those conditions that contribute to a successful outcome despite all the dire predictions to the contrary. The current focus is designed not to undermine prevention efforts but to promote social and mental health. Consistent with a positive outcome perspective, we ask: What factors, circumstances, and characteristics contribute to the teenage mother succeeding despite the odds? What can we learn from those who do?

THE CASE OF BRENDA

Her son has children of his own now, and she is working on her doctorate. Brenda's life is very different from what it appeared it would be twenty-seven years earlier. At the age of 17, Brenda had her first and only child. She quit high school to do it, lost friends, disappointed and disgraced family members, and cried.

Brenda grew up in Chester, Pennsylvania, the daughter of a construction worker and a housewife. She was the second of five children and the first daughter born to her parents. The family's small home rested on the outskirts of the housing projects. She walked home from school every day at lunchtime and then again at the end of the school day. Other children stayed at school or wandered around during their lunch period, but not Brenda: it just never occurred to her. The family did not own their home, but managed to scrape by on her father's small salary until he lost his job when Brenda was 13. The family then had to move to the heart of the projects.

Brenda shared a room with her three sisters, her brother slept downstairs on a pull-out bed, and their parents shared a room. The family still maintained a rigid routine in which the children came straight home after school, completed their cleaning chores and homework, bathed, and went to bed. The family lived strictly religious lives and were deeply involved in church activities. But Brenda says that in the projects something was different: suddenly, the family was surrounded by other people. She saw unsupervised youngsters running around outside at all hours of the night and day. In contrast, she and her siblings were closely watched. Brenda recalls that she had never before considered her parents strict, but she suddenly felt very controlled. Besides being strict, Brenda's mother was very intelligent. Brenda describes her as the type of woman who fills out crossword puzzles in ink. The house was always filled with books and magazines for the family to read, and the children, on the rare occasions when they were allowed to watch television, watched documentaries and talk shows. Television viewing was controlled by the mother.

Brenda's mother only completed her high school education, but Brenda thinks her mother's education was limited by the times, not by intelligence. Brenda explains that when her mother was growing up, a woman was expected to get married and start a family—not continue her education or have a career. Brenda's mother took great pride in her home and made sure her children were clean and fed. Years later, after her offspring had grown and left home, Brenda's mother took a job as a counselor in a school Headstart Program to help children be better prepared to learn.

Brenda was not allowed to date. She met the man who would

become her first boyfriend and the father of her child when she was 16 and going out with a group of friends to a carnival. The man, Peter, was a friend of the family, so it was acceptable for him to be visiting the house and for Brenda to go out in a group with him along. He was very sweet to Brenda and paid a lot of attention to her—a type of attention she had never received before. She hadn't been allowed to socialize with very many boys her age. Peter was 22.

They began having sex without using any form of protection against pregnancy. Brenda says she doesn't know exactly "where her head was," but she just didn't equate having sex with becoming pregnant. She says that like many teenage girls who become pregnant, she never thought it would happen to her. She had been seeing Peter for about a year, and they had sex perhaps four times when she became pregnant. She suspected her condition long before she admitted it. Her menstrual cycle had always been irregular but now had stopped completely. She also noticed that she was gaining weight on her very skinny frame. Finally, she had to acknowledge what she had suspected for some time: she was going to have a baby.

Brenda's mother reacted angrily to what she perceived as a disgrace, burden, and heartbreak Brenda had brought to the family. It was what Brenda expected and almost felt she deserved. Her father greeted the news reproachfully. "I thought you'd at least finish school," he told his daughter. She was 17 and a junior in high school. Brenda had always enjoyed a special closeness with her father; she was his first female child. Brenda, well aware that she was her father's favorite child, didn't want to lose her special place with him. Disappointing her father caused her more pain than any anger her mother could vent. She felt she had really let him down and wanted somehow to make it up to him.

In Pennsylvania in the 1950s, an unmarried teenage girl, whether from a rich or poor family, seldom became pregnant. Brenda knows only one other girl in her neighborhood who became pregnant while she was an unmarried teenager, and she did so soon after Brenda. The idea of abortion was never discussed, and Brenda never considered it. She says she knew nothing about ways to terminate a pregnancy, but it would never have been an option anyway given her religious background.

Pregnancy might as well have been leprosy in the small Pennsylvania town, and as far as Brenda's mother's family was concerned; Brenda became an outcast to her maternal family. When they spoke to her on rare occasions after she became pregnant, it was only to scorn her. Brenda's paternal family handled the whole affair differently. Brenda remembers being embraced by her paternal grandmother when she told her the news. The extended paternal family was not happy at her news, but they were more accepting. Her maternal grandfather suggested that maybe she should go away until after the baby was born, but he dropped the subject when the idea wasn't pursued.

More devastating to Brenda than her family's reaction was the rejection she felt from her friends and schoolmates. Brenda wistfully remembers her best friend announcing that she was no longer allowed to see Brenda. Brenda began to feel that people were afraid her condition and "obvious lack of morals" were contagious. But the only difference Brenda could see between herself and many of the other neighborhood girls was that she had been caught.

Of all the heartaches Brenda suffered as a result of her unexpected pregnancy, having to leave school and being unable to graduate with her class caused her the most tears. She remembers trying to get someone in her class to get her a ticket to the graduation, but all the graduates were saving their tickets for family and close friends—not for pregnant class dropouts. The night of her class's graduation, Brenda cried and pleaded but still couldn't get in. She couldn't have felt more stigmatized if a red "A" had been painted on her chest. Brenda decided that night that she would show everyone—her family and her classmates—that she was as good as, if not better than, they. She decided to finish school no matter what.

Now in her forties, Brenda says she believes her determination to get an education was 35 percent desire to further herself but 65 percent wanting to show everyone she could do it. First, she had to get through the pregnancy, which wasn't easy from the very beginning. Her son Marcus was born two months prematurely and had to spend the first 30 days of his life in a hospital incubator. So tiny that he wore doll clothes for the first few months of his life, he suffered some respiratory problems in his youth.

Brenda's mother, who had been angry since the announcement of her daughter's pregnancy, became increasingly tense when the baby was brought home. Brenda was blamed for all the problems in the house; no matter what or how small, it wouldn't have happened if Brenda hadn't gotten pregnant. Her father on the other hand, was very supportive, both emotionally and financially. Marcus would come to call him "Daddy." Brenda remembers how one year her father spent his small Christmas bonus on a walker for baby Marcus. Such expenditures only made her mother angrier. Even so, Brenda's mother did agree to help Brenda continue her education by watching the baby while Brenda was in class. Brenda started attending school in the evenings in a school building a few miles from her house. She would have to come home immediately after class because her mother had to get to civic or social meetings.

Peter, the father of her child whom she was still seeing, was to pick her up after school to drive her home. Often he wouldn't show up, and Brenda would have to walk home. The walk took about an hour, which would make her mother late for her meetings and even angrier at Brenda.

Five months after Marcus was born, Peter was drafted into the army. It was at this time that Brenda decided she couldn't keep up with her school work and care for the baby too. She also need to get a job to help with the family expenses. Although Brenda qualified for public assistance and could have moved out on her own and collected welfare, her father was adamantly opposed to it. So she stayed in her family home and accepted no help from the government.

For a while, Peter sent Brenda money but never enough to support her or the baby. Brenda's and Marcus's main financial support still came from Brenda's father.

Marcus entered day care when he was 14 months old and Brenda, then 18 years old, entered the work force. Her first job was as a recreation aide with the Youth Corps of the Chester County Housing Authority. A month later, money from Peter quit coming. Peter later said he'd heard that Brenda had a job and was doing fine, so he figured he'd keep his money. Brenda soon learned that she should be receiving a military allotment because her son was a military dependent. She called the army office to ask about the aid and found out that such money was indeed available, but that, in Peter's case, it was being sent to his wife and child in Georgia!

Brenda was mortified. She had no idea that Peter was married. The next time Peter called her, she confronted him with it. He very smoothly explained that the wife was ancient history and that they hadn't been together for years. It never dawned on Brenda until later that his wife couldn't have received the army money unless Peter had signed her up for it. Peter was very manipulative, and Brenda gullibly accepted his stories and excuses. He said whatever was necessary to pacify her, using the same approach he had used when they were dating and when they had sex. He had talked of marriage then, and Brenda had believed his flowery words, thinking she had found her "knight in shining armor." Now that Brenda knew he was married Peter spoke no more of marriage, but he still called on occasion and Brenda always talked to him. By now Brenda realized that he was not going to marry her and, indeed, had never intended to do so. She knew she would have to take care of herself and her son alone.

About a year later, Peter came to see Brenda again and wanted to start up again where they left off, as if nothing had happened. But Brenda knew now that Peter was the type of man who preyed on young, naive girls, too innocent to see beyond his lies and shams. She finally dismissed Peter from her life and decided she wouldn't be fooled by any man again.

Brenda's job as a recreation aide was a temporary "make-work" government job and didn't pay well. She immediately realized there was no future in it and that she needed another job. She also realized that without a diploma, a better job would be very hard to find. Since the government department for which she worked offered a high school equivalency program, she signed up. She left the Housing Authority, took a slightly better paying job with the quartermaster, and started taking classes at night. Her mother continued to babysit for her.

The courses were taught from a book and were designed to prepare the students for the GED (high school equivalency) test. The students were not given the textbook, but the teachers taught from it. Brenda was a very determined and bright student, but at the end of the first two-month class session, her teacher recommended that she continue in class rather than taking the test at that point. Brenda was hurt and angry, interpreting the teacher's refusal to send her to the test as a personal affront. Later, she learned that the teacher regularly and randomly held some students back to make sure his job was secure. If he didn't have a class, he didn't have a job. Brenda saw him only as a person telling her she could not do something. Determined to prove him wrong, she bought a copy of the preparatory book for herself and studied it. When she at last was recommended to take the test, she received the highest score in her group.

Brenda received her GED in 1967 and started working as a teaching assistant at the Opportunity Center where the GED classes were taught. She says she got the job because it was good public relations for the school to have one of its graduates there. She was shown off as an example to other students. However, she quickly noticed that the teaching assistants seemed to do all the work at the center while the teachers were paid all the money. She was very frustrated with the situation and guesses that she must have shown how she felt while at work.

One day when she muttered something about the conditions, one of the teachers overheard her. Rather than getting angry, the teacher responded that there was no reason why Brenda couldn't be a teacher at the center rather than just an assistant. Brenda considered the woman's words but didn't act on them until she had made friends with another assistant. This assistant, a divorcee, was singlehandedly raising eight children and trying to make a life for herself. Looking at her one child and relatively supportive family, Brenda decided her life wasn't so bad and that if this other woman could do for herself, so could she. The two became good friends and inspired each other. Brenda says they were both outcasts and renegades for their time and provided each other an understanding, supportive shoulder to lean on. They shared problems, took the Scholastic Aptitude Test together, and sent off college applications. Although Brenda's friend was not accepted at Cheney State University, where Brenda decided to go, she went on to a community college.

Getting into college was only the start of the battle, however. Brenda started taking classes during the day and working at the Opportunity Center at night. During her 5 P.M. lunch break, she would rush out to pick up her son at day care and take him home where her mother cared for him. Brenda would then hurry back to work. If the schedule itself wasn't hard enough, the classes were. Brenda found that GED courses don't necessarily prepare a person for college life. She had been out of school for three years and had never taken algebra and some of the other advanced courses with which she was now faced. She sought extra help from teachers and students and studied long hours into the night after work and on weekends. People don't realize just how hard school was for her, she says. Even her family, who watched her struggle and study, seemed to believe that her school experience flowed by effortlessly.

But Brenda vividly remembers the many sleepless nights that she stayed up studying while the house around her was quiet in sleep. Quitting school crossed her mind on a weekly basis. Every Friday, on her way home from school, she would say that she was never going back again, but somehow she would be right back at school on Monday morning ready to start again.

Brenda's father co-signed for her to get her first car so she could get back and forth to school and work. It was a big risk for a man who didn't have much money; what if she couldn't pay? But her father always had faith in his daughter, Brenda says. She remembers rushing to a final exam one morning and shutting her finger in the door of her car, tearing the fingernail off. She was so tired and worried about the test that she didn't notice the pain and was ready to take the exam with her finger bleeding and in need of medical help. Her friends finally talked her into going to a doctor rather than to her exam. She was allowed to make up the missed test.

In her junior year in college Brenda formed her own support system at the school. She found and befriended other students who were encountering the same problems she had had. It was comforting to be with people who understood what was going on—people to whom she could tell her problems and fears and who would listen and console her.

Brenda managed to finish school in four and a half years and graduated with a 3.8 grade point average. She said she didn't realize she had graduated so high in her class; that really hadn't been her goal. She was studying just to do her best, she said, and to create a life for herself and her son.

School had presented many difficult problems which Brenda, mercifully, had not anticipated. Had she realized how hard it would be, she might not have gone, she said. As it was, she just went ahead and did it.

Marcus was in second grade by now, and Brenda got a job as a special education teacher at a local public school. She also moved out of the house she had shared with her family for the last 13 years and got a small apartment where she and Marcus lived.

Relationships were a luxury for which Brenda did not have time during college. She spent her days studying or at work, and turned down any offers of dates or advances by men. Besides the schedule, she says, she was still very bitter at the realization of who Marcus's father really was. She still kept some of her old childhood friendships, however, and one relationship in particular.

Thanksgiving was the holiday when everyone in Brenda's neighborhood came home to meet with old friends and family. The previous Thanksgiving before she started at Cheney, a friend begged Brenda to accompany her to a bar where all the homecoming celebrants had planned to meet. Brenda was tired and did not want to go, but the friend was so adamant that Brenda finally agreed, on condition that she would go for only 15 minutes. She figured she could quiet her friend and still have an early evening. At the bar Brenda ran into Bill, a childhood buddy who'd been away in the military. The two of them conversed easily about old times, about her family, about his divorce and five children. The conversation was very friendly. Bill told Brenda he would stop by the house the next day to say hello to her family. She never expected him to keep his word, but the next day he showed up, just as he had said.

Neither Brenda nor Bill was ready for any kind of commitment, so their relationship remained close but strictly platonic through-out Brenda's college days. But soon after Brenda and Marcus moved out on their own, they were sharing their apartment with Bill. Brenda swore she would never get married, after all the heartache Peter had caused her. But after living together for eight years, Brenda and Bill finally married. Even though Marcus did grow up mostly in a house with a man in it, he never re-garded Bill as his father and instead continued to call Brenda's father, "Daddy." He referred to Bill in conversation with his friends as "my pop."

Brenda continued her education, becoming a certified drug and alcohol counselor and earning a master's degree in educa-tion. Her close ties to her family remained. Since she was the first member of her family to have any college education, she was regarded as the smart one and the person to turn to for emotional, intellectual, and/or financial help. At times the de-mands of family became too much for her, and after her father's death, she felt her life was falling apart.

Because Brenda was having emotional trouble defining her role in the lives of Bill's children, her marriage was endangered. During a regular medical checkup, Brenda's doctor noted that her blood pressure, usually high, was skyrocketing. When she told him of her stress, he sent her to a psychologist. Brenda was in therapy for a year, during which she faced many of the old problems that had been unresolved from her past, many of which she'd never admitted. Her big breakthrough came when she admitted that her father had been an alcoholic.

During Brenda's childhood, her father often came home very drunk and very late, having spent needed family money on alcohol. His regular schedule would place him at the local bar every night after work until 11 P.M., Friday nights he stayed at the bars until closing, and Saturdays, after a half-day at work, he would again go for a drink. Brenda's brothers and sisters had reacted to their father's open drunkenness by hiding when he would drive up to the house and beer cans would fall out of his car. Brenda was the one who would come to her father's aid. She would pick up the beer cans which had rolled down the driveway and help her father to bed. She berated her siblings for not coming to their father's aid.

Under therapy she finally came to realize and to remember instances when she was angry with her father for letting her down when she needed him. She remembers waiting one night for him to come home because he was supposed to pick up her new eyeglasses to replace those she'd broken. By the time he got home, the store was closed for the weekend, so Brenda had to spend three days with badly blurred vision. This was the kind of incident Brenda recalled in therapy. Now that she remembered her anger and disappointment, she was finally able to understand it and let it go.

Brenda admitted for the first time that she had lived in a dysfunctional family. Her mother never admitted that her husband was an alcoholic, and Brenda and her siblings seemed to accept their father's behavior as the norm. She now fears that members of her family are headed down the same alcoholic path as her father, in part because of their denial of their past. In her role as the designated family fixer, she says she wants to help her brothers and sisters, but they deny that they have any problems.

Brenda also worked out the anger she had for other people, including Marcus's father, and learned to handle her stress in a healthy manner, rather than just holding it in. She remains in a support group to help herself and other people like her. She is also still married but admits that the relationship, like all relationships, is one that she and her husband have to work on constantly. They have learned to discuss small problems before they have a chance to escalate.

As for her son, he is now an adult with children of his own. He finished high school and went to college for a time, but quit because he wanted to start working. Brenda refers to him as a doer, a person who works real hard. She recognizes that Marcus is basically and inherently a good person, but she never gave him a chance to go bad. Seeing how other children were growing up in the neighborhood where she lived, she wanted to keep her son out of trouble. Knowing that she had to keep Marcus fully occupied while she was in school, she signed him up for groups and classes so that he would be super busy—just like his mother. She also formed a network of parents with young children in her neighborhood who took turns carpooling them to a variety of events and babysitting for each other.

Marcus was a member of the Boy Scouts, church groups, and school clubs. When he was 12, he started babysitting in the neighborhood to earn some money; a few years later, he got a job and contributed to household expenses.

Brenda says that when Marcus was born she decided that he would have the best. There was no reason that this child should suffer for any mistakes she had made in the past. And she kept her word. She recalls only once when she was disappointed in her son. When he was 17 years old, Marcus came to her to tell her he had gotten a girl pregnant. The news was most disappointing to Brenda because she had always been open to him about sex and its possible repercussions. When he was younger she had taken him to the drug store and shown him a condom display and told him which ones to buy. She even left money for him to use if he needed it to buy the condoms. She said he knew how to avoid a pregnancy.

From the first day of the child's life, Marcus worked to care for his son. Because he had never known his own father, Marcus wanted very much to be a part of his son's life. From the day the child was born, Marcus was there providing financial and emotional support. He and the mother now live together with their two children.

Brenda speaks with pride of her son's life and her grandchildren. Her son is basically a good person, she repeats. She is sure that if she had stayed with Marcus's father her life and her son's life would have turned out very differently. Brenda works in school system administration now and has started working on her doctorate in education. She says the degree is something she must do for herself. She will then have finally proven to herself and the rest of the world that she can do anything she puts her mind to.

Brenda attributes her life success to both luck and hard work. She admits she was simply in the right place at the right time for some of the opportunities she has had, but nothing has come easy. She also credits her success to her faith in God. Attending church regularly, she prays for help with all her problems.

Brenda states that young women who become pregnant today aren't as stigmatized as she was in her day, but they still face many problems. She believes they, too, can succeed, if they are determined, willing to work, and have strong support. Brenda can't imagine what she would have done without strong support from her father, who also fulfilled a father's role for her son. Brenda's father also provided financial help, such as lunch money for Marcus and helping Brenda get a loan for a car so she could get back and forth to school and job. Although her mother held a lot of anger for Brenda and was disappointed with her, she also helped her a great deal by taking care of Marcus and by letting Brenda live in the house until she finished school and could support herself.

Brenda volunteers her time with a counseling center near her home and tries to help as many troubled youth as she can spot. She has conquered her own anger, financial problems, poor background, and emotional problems, but, again, she says it was not easy. "Success is hard work."

A SEARCH FOR SIGNIFICANT FACTORS

For Brenda, success has meant hard work. Unlike many of her counterparts, she has overcome the stigmatization associated with being a high school dropout, "pregnant teenager," and "housing project resident" to claim educational, social, and economic success. While she had to contend with a significant amount of family dysfunction during her formative years, she was not prevented from obtaining the level of success she now enjoys. Without question, she has experienced some personal problems as a result of the multiple stressful conditions surrounding her development. As suggested in an earlier volume, "Resilient children are those who, because of stressful life events, are at risk of developing later psychological dysfunctions, but do not" (Rhodes and Brown, 1991, p. 1). Given Brenda's significant personal problems attributable to family dysfunction—problems requiring psychological intervention— many may not consider Brenda a "resilient child," using Rhodes and Brown's definition of resiliency. Rhodes and Brown continue: "As example: every teenage parent does not quit school and live on welfare; most behavioral disordered children do not become dysfunctional adults; not all high school dropouts fail to make a good living; and many adjudicated delinquents do not become adult offenders" (p. 1).

To some extent, Brenda's case, probably more than any of the others discussed in this volume, may not be considered a clear-cut case of "succeeding despite the odds." However, Brenda has succeeded, far surpassing the bleak predictions suggested at the beginning of this chapter and beyond what most people would have expected. In our view, obtaining such success qualifies Brenda as an individual who "succeeded despite the odds." The question we want to address now is: What factors contributed to her success?

Parental Influence

Although Brenda eventually discovered that she had been raised in a dysfunctional family, her family was not without structure, rituals, and moral development. Brenda described the importance of religion and church involvement in her development, and she emphasized that her parents were very strict, always keeping a watchful eye out for their children. The children were expected to do chores, homework, and be well groomed. While their home, in the heart of the housing projects, was obviously overcrowded, with six people living in two bedrooms and kids doubling up in beds, the mother took pride in their home and made sure the children were clean and well fed. Television watching was closely supervised, and books and magazines were always available for reading. Brenda's mother was described as very intelligent, and her father was pictured as emotionally and financially supportive, one who considered Brenda very special. Despite its reported dysfunctional nature, the family remained intact and, to some extent, appeared to provide a nourishing environment for Brenda. She was in her junior year in high school and did not exhibit any serious educational, social, and/or emotional problems.

Both parents reacted negatively to their daughter's pregnancy—the mother with anger, the father with hurt and disappointment. The community also disapproved. The negative reactions by these socializing agents seem to have served as a stimulus propelling Brenda toward success and toward proving that she was "as good, if not better than what they say." Brenda believes that this "I'll show them" attitude has been a major factor contributing to her current level of educational achievement.

Despite the financial hardship that Brenda's pregnancy placed on her family, her father would not allow her to go on welfare and, within his means, gave her needed financial assistance. While clearly disapproving of Brenda's pregnancy, her mother helped by providing needed cost-free babysitting.

The Influence of an Inspiring Relationship

Brenda's relationship with a divorcee proved inspiring and supportive. The divorcee's attempt to improve her own life situation, under more difficult circumstances, caused Brenda to believe that she could do the same. While the divorcee was obviously older and much more experienced in life than Brenda, the two shared a bond and a supportive relationship that was mutually beneficial.

The Influence of a Support Group

Brenda received much needed help from several support groups. At college, she developed an informal support group that provided needed support and understanding, and in the neighborhood she formed a network with other mothers which helped with babysitting and transportation needs.

Personality Factors

Interview data clearly indicate that Brenda is an extremely determined individual. Once stimulated towards achievement, she worked extremely hard to succeed, which undoubtedly required a tremendous amount of discipline and determination. While we may not be able to directly measure the determination associated with the "I'll show them" attitude, which seems to possess Brenda, we can say that this attitude propelled her toward goal attainment. Although hard work and determination contribute to academic success, her graduating from college with such a high grade point average attests to her intellectual potential.

For the most part, Brenda's personality test scores indicate that she is basically an average person, though she is considered warm, good natured, and easy to get along with. In addition, she is characterized as extremely self-sufficient, a trait that may have developed out of necessity or, if inherited, helped support her achievements. In any event, those who score well on the self-sufficiency scale tend to do well educationally. Personality test scores also indicate that Brenda is tense and driven—characteristics that could serve her well if channeled appropriately.

Generally, Brenda can be described as a warm, intelligent, well-educated, hardworking, self-sufficient individual, who is continually striving to maximize her potential both personally and professionally. She has defied the odds, despite her status as a teenage parent, a high school dropout, and a housing project resident. Factors that appeared significant to Brenda's achievement were a supportive parental and friendship network, intellectual potential, and a determined "I'll show them" attitude.

CHAPTER SEVEN

Abandoning a Delinquent Lifestyle to Become Successful: A Self-Analysis

Every year an alarming number of children commit criminal acts, ranging from crimes against persons, such as rape and robbery, to crimes against property, such as burglary and automobile theft. Some of these youthful offenders are caught and placed in juvenile facilities for detention and treatment. Since its inception, the juvenile court has focused on treating rather than punishing the juvenile offender, thus differentiating it from the adult justice system. The comparative leniency of the juvenile justice system has caused many to question whether the youthful offenders are literally getting away with murder.

Research suggests that many of the adults found in this country's correctional institutions began their criminal careers as juveniles. Typically, these incarcerated adults did poorly in school, eventually dropped out and became more involved in delinquent activities, and ultimately were arrested and confined in juvenile facilities. Eventually, the individual graduates into the adult criminal justice system either by simply getting older or upon committing an offense for which he is tried as an adult. This theory of a spiral from childhood misconduct to adult criminal behavior has been described as the "path of progressive deterioration" (Rhodes, Duncan, and Hall, 1987).

As a first step in preventing delinquency and short-circuiting the destructive progression from juvenile to adult crime, delinquency research has concentrated on identifying factors that contribute to delinquency involvement. Much of this work is aimed at identifying differences between those individuals who become delinquent and those who do not. However, there appears to be no clear consensus on what factors promote the onset of delinquent involvement or its maintenance. Many theories abound. Neither do we have a clear definition of the factors that halt the delinquency spiral. Some delinquents are never apprehended or adjudicated, but nonetheless terminate delinquent behavior, just as effectively as do some delinquents who do become involved with the juvenile justice system.

What causes a juvenile delinquent to abandon delinquency? Our interviewee for this case study reports a pattern of delinquency including arrest and detention in a juvenile facility and incarceration in an adult institution—all occurring before the age of 18. But thereafter the individual reports no further delinquency and demonstrates adaptation to a successful, noncriminal lifestyle extending well into adulthood. Because it is the general perception that most juvenile offenders who are arrested and incarcerated continue their criminal behavior well into adulthood, the juvenile who abandons a delinquent lifestyle has truly "beaten the odds." What can we learn from this individual?

THE CASE OF WARREN

The banging downstairs was so loud that 11-year-old Warren and his younger sister, Jean, huddled in an upstairs bedroom, sure the house was being robbed. Their older brother, Sonny, had left earlier in the day, and their parents were at work. It was one of many unchaperoned days during summer vacation from school. The children found nothing to eat except some leftover beans; Sonny refused to eat that, but Warren and Jean ate them hungrily. Sonny left the house.

The banging got louder. Warren was terrified, but it was his responsibility to find out what was happening. He forced Jean to hide in a closet while he slowly and cautiously crept down the stairs.

"Meaty!" Sonny's familiar voice called Warren's nickname,

but added no reassurance. Whoever was breaking into the house had caught Sonny and was torturing him, Warren thought.

Running to help his brother, Warren found that the noise and his brother's voice were coming from outside the front door. Warren threw the door open to discover his brother being held by two big men. These men were not burglars, however; they were police officers. They said Sonny had been caught trying to steal some buns from a bakery. The noise that had so frightened Warren and Jean resulted from the police banging on the door with their nightsticks; why they didn't just ring the doorbell Warren couldn't figure out. This was the first time Warren had seen a police officer up close.

Warren was the second of three children, all of whom were very nearly the same age. Sonny, Warren, and Jean were very close as children, Warren said, partly because they shared a bedroom for a long time. The other two rooms were occupied by the children's parents and a boarder.

Despite the children's closeness, Warren does not describe his family life as either warm or loving. His father never touched or held him and, in fact, had very little to do with the children unless he was undermining the mother's authority. During the week, Warren's father worked hard as a janitor at a convent. He was a model employee: conscientious, prompt, reliable, and cooperative. But after work every Friday—payday–he would get staggeringly drunk and would stay drunk through Sunday afternoon.

Warren recalls no affection between his parents, but he clearly remembers the countless, pointless arguments that always degenerated into physical beatings. Warren and the other children had all been injured several times in attempting to stop their father from beating their mother.

Warren never really understood why his mother endured such abuse. She was certainly no weak, dependent pushover. As a teenager, she had left her parents' poor, rural North Carolina home to work as a welder in the Norfolk, Virginia, shipyards. In 1953, when she realized that her young family was seriously endangered by her husband's drinking and nefarious activities, she singlehandedly moved her husband and children to Baltimore for a fresh start. Since then, she had done everything she possibly could to make ends meet—from working several house-keeping jobs simultaneously to taking in boarders. She taught her children the value of money and showed them how to sacrifice toward financial goals. And although the house was furnished mostly with second-hand, well-used stuff, the family owned their home. Warren took pride in his family's home ownership and knew it resulted from his mother's ingenuity and determination to stretch the family's poor income as far as humanly possible. From what Warren could see, his mother was certainly capable of managing—even getting along better—without his father.

But Warren's mother was deeply religious and believed she was duty-bound to stand by her husband, no matter what. So, she and the children endured the endless conflict.

Warren's father was illiterate and deliberately uninvolved with his children. Sitting in front of the television set every night, not bothering to eat dinner with the family, he would instruct his children to take all of their problems and requests to their mother. However, on many occasions he overruled her decisions by instructing the children to do exactly the opposite.

Warren's mother almost always yielded to her husband, even when his decision was clearly inappropriate. The children often took advantage of the parents' disunity. They hated attending Sunday School, so they appealed to their father when their mother insisted they go. In this, she would not yield, and the children would go to Sunday School only after she had paid dearly in humiliation and aggravation. She was committed to having her children raised with Christian values. Warren's father would also countermand punishments his wife meted out to the children. Warren remembers coming home on one occasion after getting into a fight at school. Warren had started the fight, but his intended victim bested him in the confrontation. His mother confined Warren to the house to punish his behavior, but his father sent Warren back out to find the other kid with the intent of winning the fight this time.

Despite their parents' marital difficulties, Sonny, Warren, and Jean seemed happy and reasonably well adjusted. They all did well in school, particularly Sonny.

Warren idolized Sonny. To Warren, big brother was everything Warren wanted to be—handsome, witty, popular, and intelligent. Sonny seemed content with his role as the revered eldest son and positive role model for his siblings—that is, until Buddy and Leroy came into the picture. Buddy, 17, and his brother Leroy, 16, moved into Warren's home after their father— Warren's uncle—died suddenly, leaving the boys completely without adult supervision. Buddy and Leroy shared Warren's bedroom. Changes in the boys and the household began immediately. For example, the tight bond that had always existed between Warren and his brother and sister began to disintegrate. Buddy and Leroy were smart to the ways of the streets and were eager to teach Warren and Sonny everything they knew. The bedroom became a classroom where Buddy and Leroy taught Sonny and Warren all they needed to know about being "bad dudes."

Before Buddy and Leroy moved in, neither Sonny nor Warren had shown any delinquent tendencies. Sonny's one run-in with the police could even be explained in somewhat socially acceptable terms in that he was stealing only out of hunger. But under Buddy's and Leroy's tutelage, stealing was done for stealing's sake.

The first lesson the cousins taught was that fights were to be won—at all cost. Warren and Sonny watched their cousins dress to attend parties every Friday and Saturday night. Because the night would inevitably end in a fight, the evening's attire always included a knife, strategically placed for easy access. Buddy and Leroy always practiced a couple of draws before leaving—just to be sure. Buddy and Leroy also gave lessons in wine drinking, stealing, shooting craps, going to jail, and "making it" with women. Sonny changed first. He started talking back to his mother, getting into trouble in school, fighting, and doing whatever else he could do to be like Buddy and Leroy. In addition, money and other items started to disappear from the house.

Twelve-year-old Warren was truly fascinated by his cousins' exciting lifestyle, but he was still reluctant to join them. Warren had a paper route, delivering 100 newspapers every weekday and 200 on Sunday. It had been Sonny's paper route, but Sonny gave it up because Buddy and Leroy didn't think it was "manly" enough. Warren enjoyed spending the money he earned from his route but found he had to hide his money or it would disappear during the night.

At Christmas time Warren made extra money because his customers gave him generous tips for a year of faithful service. This year, 1960, he had made more than $20 in tips. To a 12 year old that was a fortune. He knew he had to guard it, so at night he put it in a sock which he wore to bed. But in the morning, Warren's money was gone. Someone had cut a hole in his sock while he slept and removed the cash. Sonny, Buddy, and Leroy were laughing about the theft as Warren awoke. Warren never found out who took the money but remembers feeling totally defeated. Warren decided then and there that since he obviously couldn't beat them, he would join them. Besides, Warren reasoned, what rewards was he given for being a "good" kid? He saw that his brother, though in trouble most of the time, still got treats from their mother, even expensive shoes or clothing. Warren, on the other hand, felt that he was often asked to wait or was denied material requests altogether.

First, Warren started picking up any money he found unattended—at home, school, church, stores, in pockets, wallets, and purses. Even if he was caught, his punishment was always the same: he would be beaten and then the incident would be forgotten. Later, Warren quit his paper route and started carrying a club to help in the frequent fights he started. After spending more time in the principal's office than in the classroom and doing nothing constructive when he did make an appearance before a teacher, Warren failed sixth grade.

Warren's parents, finally realizing Buddy's and Leroy's terrible influence on Warren and Sonny, put them out of their house; but by then it was too late. Sonny and Warren had learned so much about being "bad" that they didn't need their "teachers" any more.

A week before finishing seventh grade, Warren was expelled from school for extorting money from other children. His actions were not without consequence to his family. His mother's job was jeopardized because she was so frequently called to school or the police station during the workday owing to either Sonny or Warren being in trouble—again. According to Warren, he knew his deeds were hard on the family, but he couldn't resist the flash of his new lifestyle. Warren's orientation had completely changed. Whereas he once cared deeply about making his mother proud, now he was more interested in being the leader of his gang of friends. He still wanted the same things—respect and admiration—but from a different audience and for different reasons.

Everything Warren did was designed to achieve status in the subculture he now embraced: he fought to prove his toughness; he stole to prove his skill and daring. By the time he was 14, he had cultivated a look, walk, and vocabulary to tell the world just how "bad" he was.

It was at about this time that Sonny was arrested for stealing a coat and was sent to the Maryland Training School for Boys. Warren was scared for his brother. Reportedly, only the worst boys were sent to the Training School; Warren had heard rumors of boys being robbed, beaten, and sexually molested there. But Sonny returned triumphant. He told exciting stories about the Training School: tales of riots, escape plots, and fights filled Warren with envy and a desire to be part of it.

Warren and his friends now decided that they, too, wanted to be "rehabilitated." They stole, set fires, broke and entered, and got into whatever trouble they could get into. Although the boys were not sloppy in their actions, they weren't afraid of being caught either. Eventually, they were caught and ordered to appear in court. The boys made a pact that they would do whatever it took to get into juvenile detention. Warren was to curse the judge so there would be no pity on him.

On the trial day, Warren's mother dressed him neatly. He remembers her tucking in his shirt just before they were to enter the courtroom. As soon as she turned her back he pulled his shirt out again. His mother looked so afraid for him that he tried to console her, but he would not let his friends down. He was so belligerent to the judge that he was sent to the Maryland Children's Center. His friends were sent to other institutions.

Warren's six weeks in the detention center were basically uneventful, but when he returned home, his stories were just as grand and glorious as any of Sonny's. Warren's stint in detention made him appear even tougher than before in the eyes of his young protégés.

Warren's deviant behavior continued. One night he and a friend broke into a storefront residence where a gun and some money were supposed to be kept. Without a thought that someone could be home and he could be killed, Warren ran directly to the bedroom, where he began his search for the gun. He was about to give up when his hand struck metal under the mattress. Warren grabbed the gun—a .38 caliber pistol—found his friend downstairs, and together they ran.

Having the gun took Warren's ego to new heights. One night he aimed the gun at a friend and told him to run. Warren took careful aim and shot! The friend fell down and, for a moment, Warren panicked; he hadn't really expected to hit his friend. When his friend got up and continued running, Warren's panic subsided.

A week later the friend who helped Warren break into the store brought some younger boys to Warren's home to see the gun. "They don't believe we have a gun," Harry said. "Let them see." So Warren took the boys to the basement where the gun was hidden. He was angry that Harry had referred to it as "their gun," and wanted to teach him a lesson. There was one bullet in the gun, and Warren placed it where he thought it wouldn't be fired. He decided a good scare was what these boys needed. He pointed the gun directly at the boys, and two of them left immediately. With a deadly serious face to hide the hysterical laughter he felt inside, Warren began to threaten the two remaining boys in the basement to make sure they knew the gun was his alone. Finally, he turned the gun toward one of the boys—an 11 year old named Marcus—and slowly pulled the trigger, expecting to hear the click of an empty chamber. BANG! The force of the bullet threw Marcus across the room where he clutched his stomach, screaming, and then fell to the floor with his eyes closed.

Warren was taken away in a police wagon as neighbors watched and pointed fingers. He left not knowing if he had killed Marcus, but he knew that, having turned 16 the month before, he would be treated as an adult. Fear grew inside him as he was frisked and put in a holding cell. He decided to hang himself from the ceiling with his belt, but after three attempts, he found he was too tall and gave up.

Soon Warren was taken to Baltimore City Jail where he would await trial. Three adults accompanied him in the patrol wagon to jail. They all had killed someone with a gun. They assured Warren that, if he shot a kid in the chest at close range with a .38, the kid was dead. "You got yourself a murder rap kid," one of the men said.

At this point Warren's life might have changed. He had never considered himself a murderer and didn't like the feeling. He wanted something different. His mother came to visit him at jail but could only offer Jesus as the answer to his present situation. She insisted that Warren must pray to the Lord for forgiveness. Warren prayed to Jesus that Marcus would not die and that he would not go to jail. He spent 21 days in Baltimore City Jail where he was beaten and his clothes stolen; he had no idea whether Marcus was dead or alive. The only thing he knew was that prison was not for him.

Marcus lived, recovering almost completely while Warren was in jail. He spoke on Warren's behalf at the trial. Warren was sentenced to six months in Baltimore City Jail, but the judge gave him a suspended sentence with two years of probation. When Warren was released from jail, his mother reminded him that it was Jesus who answered his prayers.

Whenever Warren would get into trouble, he always prayed to Jesus as his mother had instructed him. In prayer, he asked the Lord, "If you get me out of this one, I promise I will not get into any more trouble." Once out of trouble, however, he invariably forgot his promise.

After getting out of jail, Warren decided he was too old for school. His father had never seen much point in it and didn't care if the children finished or not. He thought they should be working for their living anyway. Although she would have preferred Warren to finish high school, his mother saw no stigma in having her son quit. Warren started looking for a job, but without even an eighth grade education, his opportunities were extremely limited. He soon became discouraged and eventually quit looking altogether. His favorite pastime became sitting on the front step of a neighborhood store with some friends, making a lot of noise and harassing the store owner. For his part, the store owner hired a security guard and threatened to have Warren arrested. The fear of jail didn't slow down the harassment, just Warren's blatant part in it. He resorted to setting up situations and having others do the work.

One night, Warren convinced one of his buddies to throw a bottle at the security guard. While Warren hadn't actually thrown the bottle, he was arrested for the attempted assault. Witnesses came to court to testify they had seen him throw the bottle. Warren was sentenced to six months in Baltimore City Jail, with the possibility of another six months being tacked on for violating his probation. Life in jail the second time around was worse than the first. An inmate picked a fight with Warren soon after he arrived, and both young men were put in solitary confinement. Warren was kept alone in a small dark cell and given only bread and water to eat.

The day after his release from solitary, Warren was right back in, being blamed for noise an inmate on another level of the prison was making. For this second stint, he was placed in a one-person cell already occupied by several other men. Warren remembers feeling the hostility building toward him in the cell because the men were angry and he was from a different side of town than they. Warren recalls praying to the Lord to help him out of this situation. He was saved only because a young white man was thrown in the cell and Warren was taken out. That evening Warren heard the screams of the white man as the others beat him mercilessly and then sexually molested him. Warren knew how close he had come to being that screaming victim. Because Warren was the only inmate removed from the cell, he believed that his prayers were answered again.

Warren was one of the youngest inmates and realized that many of the older inmates had probably started out as he did at a young age. But Warren didn't use his time to do any serious reflection on his life situation; at 17, he returned to the streets prepared to continue where he'd left off.

One night, Warren was shooting up drugs with Sonny. It was the first time Warren had handled the syringe himself. After pumping in the heroin, he kept depressing the plunger and would probably have killed himself by injecting air into his vein if Sonny hadn't stopped him.

Warren started to feel he wasn't in control of his life. He realized there were many aspects of being a "bad dude," such as using drugs, with which he never wanted to become involved. In the end, however, he did whatever was necessary to build up his tough image. Warren was indeed a "bad dude," but if he had any problems, he could always call on God, and sometimes his older brother, to take care of him.

About a week after the drug injection incident, Warren got into another of his many fights, but this time, the other dude's gang chased him. Warren found his brother and, with the help of Sonny's gang, tracked down the other group. The fight began. Suddenly a shot rang out and Sonny fell to the ground. He had been shot in the head and was nearly killed.

Almost killing himself was one thing, but nearly causing his brother's death was the last straw. Warren knew he had to change his life. He believed that God would eventually stop saving him from trouble and that he would eventually have to "pay." But it was difficult for him to change even though he wanted to. Warren knew he couldn't do it alone, and he couldn't do it in his old environment. It was then that he heard about the Job Corps, which would give him a chance to learn a skill. Because Warren had a criminal record, he thought that he would not be accepted in the Job Corps. He prayed and begged the recruiting officer to accept him into the program. After he was accepted, he was told that in three months he would depart for the Job Corps center in Breckenridge, Kentucky.

Whether or not opportunities had been available before, Warren had never seen them. Like an alcoholic, there was no way he could have been helped until he first committed himself to change. Warren says he had reached a window of vulnerability where help could get to him. He spent most of his three-month waiting period in the safety of his house. He knew that if he went out, he would get into trouble, get caught, and lose his chance.

Warren wanted to do good, but the delinquent lifestyle had taken years to build, as had his place of authority in it. It was hard to discard it overnight. When several friends from the old neighborhood joined him in the Job Corps and invited him to join in their deviant behavior, he did so because he felt he couldn't say no. He said his friends never put any pressure on him; the pressure was created inside himself.

A Job Corps staff member caught Warren sniffing glue and abusing cough medicine. Although these infractions justified immediate expulsion from the Corps, the staff member didn't turn him in. Instead, the counselor used the threat of exposure and expulsion as a constant reminder to Warren that he'd better "walk the straight and narrow." This threat worked because, despite Warren's lapse into destructive behaviors, his goals had truly begun to change from wanting to maintain himself as a "bad dude," to wanting to make his family proud. His imagining the day he would cross the stage for his certificate with his family cheering in the background kept him working toward his Job Corps graduation.

One of Warren's classroom teachers took an interest in him, tutoring him and making him feel that she really believed in him and wanted him to do well in the Job Corps. When he didn't give his all, she would be disappointed. For Warren this teacher's approval became very important; he worked to make her proud of him, just as he wanted his mother to be proud of him.

As his graduation date, neared, Warren started to feel he was gaining control of his life. A test of his newfound control came when another corpsman tried to pick a fight with him. Rather than fight, Warren first tried to defuse the situation and eventually just walked away, while his would-be attacker called him "chicken." For the first time in six years, Warren had turned his back on a fight, proving to himself that he did indeed control his life.

Warren received his Job Corps certificate in retail sales; he was inundated with congratulations from family, friends, and Job Corps personnel, and with an enormous, unaccustomed feeling of gratitude and self-satisfaction. But he wanted more. Warren decided to go after his high school diploma, which would be a difficult task. He had never even finished eighth grade, so he had five years of high school to make up. He also had to make a living. But Warren found that he now approached the challenge of completing his education with the same energy and excitement he once had for planning a robbery or winning a fight. His Job Corps training enabled him to get a stock clerk's position with a big Baltimore retailer. He attended night school every night for two years and worked very hard at his studies.

As Warren drew nearer to receiving his high school diploma, he started dreaming about going to college, and he shared that dream with one of his night school teachers. The teacher discouraged Warren by saying he just wasn't "college material." While these words were very disheartening, it made him determined to prove them wrong.

Amazingly, Warren got the most encouragement from some of the "bad dudes" with whom he used to spend time during his delinquent days. As he walked to night school, he would run into old friends loitering on the streets—doing the same things he used to do. They would shout to him words of praise and envy for what he was doing with his life. Somewhere along the line, Warren had become a good example. Warren could not understand why his old buddies were not trying to improve their lives like he was doing. He decided that he would definitely go to college and study psychology to discover how he could help "bad dudes" change like he was doing. With the determination to prove his night school teacher wrong and to help his buddies, Warren took not only his B.S. degree in psychology, but his M.S., and Ph.D. as well.

Today Warren is living the kind of life his mother dreamed of for him when he was very young. He is a professor of psychology at Delaware State College in Dover, Delaware, where he lives with his wife and daughter. He has written several publications on delinquency and its abandonment. He has also written two plays that have been presented several times in the Maryland/Delaware area and is active in his church. One of the highlights of Warren's career came when he was asked to speak about his experiences at a White House conference chaired by First Lady Rosalynn Carter. It was the topic of a short book he wrote called "From the Jailhouse to the White House."

As a psychologist, Warren recognizes that many theories of treatment have proven successful in rehabilitating a delinquent, once he or she has decided to change. He says that, while other factors are important, such as opportunities, breaks, and divine intervention, he emphasizes that the decision to change must be made first. If his assessment is accurate, Sonny must not have decided to change, for he was recently released on parole from a 40-year prison sentence, after serving over 16 years.

Warren firmly believes there is hope; delinquency can be turned around. The first step, however, is to decide to change and to be determined.

A SEARCH FOR SIGNIFICANT FACTORS

Many sociologists and psychologists believe that criminal behavior is learned, and such would seem to be the case for Warren. The idea is best described by the differential association theory (Sutherland, 1947); that is, one learns to be criminal through association and communication with someone who embraces the criminal lifestyle. The person also learns how to commit a crime and how to rationalize the crime. In Warren's case, all the association and communication needed took place with his cousins in the small bedroom. Lessons were detailed, sometimes including visual aids. While the differential association theory may apply to Warren, there are several theories of why a child becomes a delinquent; much less, however, is known about why a child abandons a delinquent lifestyle.

Warren demonstrated a delinquent lifestyle that included engaging in delinquent conduct, being arrested, serving time in jail, and using drugs. Warren's delinquent lifestyle is characteristic of a significant number of adult criminals, but he completely abandoned his delinquent lifestyle prior to his majority to excel academically and become a productive law-abiding citizen. Delinquency prevention must always be the primary goal for the juvenile justice system. However, if a youth becomes involved in a delinquent lifestyle, the juvenile justice system must understand strategies that help the youth abandon that lifestyle and become a productive citizen. Much can be learned from studying the life of one who did. Warren is one who abandoned a delinquent lifestyle to succeed despite the odds. What factors were important in creating and maintaining his turnaround?

Mother's Influence

Warren's mother is described as a deeply religious woman. She raised her children with Christian values and particularly encouraged Warren to pray to Jesus to help him get out of trouble. When trouble was averted, she would remind her son that it was Jesus who helped him. As a result of his mother's teachings on Christian values, Warren prayed to Jesus and believed that it was Jesus who was protecting him from danger and helping him stay out of trouble. Consistent with his Christian orientation, Warren believed that he had a responsibility to behave in a Christian manner or he would have to "pay" for not doing so, particularly since Jesus had helped him so. Whether the breaks that Warren received were a result of divine intervention or just plain luck is debatable; what is important is that Warren believed that he was being helped by Jesus and, as a result, tried to conform his behavior to match Christian ideals.

His mother also taught her children to sacrifice for financial goals, while both parents, through example, taught the importance of hard work. Undoubtedly, these latter values helped Warren in succeeding once he made up his mind to do so.

Potentially Fatal Events

Two potentially fatal events occurring within a week of each other proved particularly important in Warren's decision to change his life for the better. Nearly killing himself while shooting drugs and starting a fight that resulted in Sonny being shot in the head both combined to make Warren believe he was not in control of his life and that something terrible was going to happen to him or someone he loved if he didn't change. Warren believes that prior to these two potentially fatal events, all attempts to improve his life had been superficial. It was now or never, he thought.

External Resources—the Job Corps

Once Warren decided that he had to change his life, he signed up and was accepted in the Job Corps. The Job Corps program gave Warren the opportunity to receive skills training in a different social environment, away from the social pressures he felt he could not resist. Two Job Corps staff members were particularly helpful in Warren's succeeding in the program. Instead of reporting Warren's abuse of glue and cough syrup—events that would most certainly have resulted in Warren's expulsion from Job Corps—the counselors used the threat of expulsion as a means of keeping Warren in line. One Job Corps teacher took an interest in him and encouraged him in his studies. Warren found himself working hard in the program to receive this teacher's approval. He began imagining himself graduating from the Job Corps while family members cheered his accomplishments. These images, according to Warren, helped motivate him and kept him working toward that goal. Once Warren graduated from the Job Corps, he felt such a great sense of accomplishment that he developed a goal—graduating from high school—and yearned for the accompanying feelings of accomplishment. For Warren, success truly bred success.

Positive and Negative Motivation

Warren was initially discouraged by his night school teacher's assessment of his college potential, but eventually Warren used this negative event as a source of motivation. He was determined to prove to this teacher that he was wrong. Warren was also motivated by his old buddies, who praised him for his efforts at changing and improving his life. He was so moved by his old buddies' support for him that he became even more determined to attend college and study psychology so he could help his buddies and others like them to change and improve their lives. In addition, Warren's experiences in jail were unpleasant; that is, some of his personal property was stolen, several times he was placed in solitary confinement, he came extremely close to being sexually molested, and so on. These experiences motivated Warren to avoid being reincarcerated.

Personality Factors

Personality assessments indicate that Warren is an unconventional, very tense, and driven individual. He tends to be insecure and is easily upset, and he is characterized as independent and self-directed, with an orientation toward establishing control over his environment. Feeling a sense of losing control over his life was a major reason Warren, as a youth, felt he had to make a change in his life. In addition, he is described as imaginative and creative, characteristics that also undoubtedly served him well, for he reported being motivated by an active imagination. Interestingly, Warren's personality characteristics are very consistent with his current occupation and avocation—college professor and playwright.

A combination of personal characteristics and orientation, established Christian ethics, divine intervention and/or luck, and supportive external motivation all contributed to Warren's succeeding despite the odds.

CHAPTER EIGHT

Why Some Children Succeed Despite the Odds

The major purpose of this volume is to elucidate those factors that help children succeed despite the odds. But just what does "succeeding despite the odds" mean? While the phrase is used often, researchers have not agreed on a universally accepted definition. Defining such a concept, however, would start with a definition of success, which itself is very subjective. Our participants were identified because they had experienced some devastating, potentially debilitating childhood circumstance, but they triumphed to become extraordinarily productive adults. Many factors may be used in defining success. Academic achievement was the primary factor used in selecting our participants: they all demonstrated a high level of academic success, as evidenced by their achieving at least the master's degree, four receiving their doctorate. All participants are working in high-level positions in their respective professions. We will not attempt to articulate the many other dimensions on which our participants succeeded. In this regard, we will allow the reader to make his or her own assessment. However, we believe that, after reading their stories, the reader will agree that our participants have indeed succeeded despite the odds.

Of course, when selecting our participants, we were not aware of all the specifics of their lives. Naively, we started our investigation thinking that our participants thrived without any real ill effects. We were wrong. We learned that all of our participants, to some degree, experienced some ill effects as a result of their childhood experiences. These effects varied emotionally, behaviorally, socially, and so on, depending on the individual and accompanying life circumstances. However, these ill effects were not devastating and are not peculiar to our participants; they also occur in the lives of individuals who have endured other kinds of life crises. Our participants can be best described as "resilient" rather than "invulnerable." That is, they were able to satisfactorily compensate for and rebound from the negative effects of their childhood experiences as opposed to escaping from them unscathed. Indeed, some researchers indicate that such adaptive behavior is an integral part of healthy development (Richardson, Neiger, Jensen, and Kumpfer, 1990).

While we tried to identify individuals who experienced certain potentially debilitating life circumstances (e.g., parental divorce or living in foster care), our investigation revealed that several participants actually experienced additional potentially debilitating life circumstances, such as extensive parental discord, parental emotional disturbance, parental alcoholism, and sibling death. These factors provide additional support for the case that these individuals succeeded despite the odds, and they make it impossible to neatly place our participants into discrete categories. We believe this latter finding occurs not only in our small pool of participants, but also in group investigations with large members of participants. Thus, investigators must be careful when categorizing individuals on the basis of particular life circumstances.

In the beginning of our investigation, we asked, "Who are those individuals who have succeeded despite the odds?" As indicated by an objective personality test, our participants demonstrated very different personality profiles, varying widely on individual characteristics, as well as on a composite of characteristics that reportedly provides a better overall picture of the individual's personality than do individual characteristics. When we looked closely at individual characteristics on which participants were similar, we found that six participants scored extremely high on the Abstract Thinking, Venturesome, and

Suspicious characteristics. Five participants scored extremely high on the Self-sufficient, Tense/Driven, Forthright, and Sensitive characteristic, while four participants scored extremely high on the Dominant, Experimenting, and Conscientious characteristics. The seven participants varied considerably on all other individual characteristics.

Although not all participants scored extremely high on it, the Sensitive characteristic is the only one common to all participants. It has been suggested that high scorers on this scale tend to be daydreamers, dependent, overprotected, insecure, temperamental, and unrealistic. While other characteristics are certainly important, one must be, to some extent, an *unrealistic daydreamer* to succeed despite the odds. Indeed, Warren indicated that his active imagination helped him to continue working hard towards achieving his goals.

Referring to the Venturesome characteristic, one authority in personality assessment (Krug, 1981) stated:

[There appears to be] an analogy between scores on this factor and the degree of psychological "insulation" the individual possesses. High-scoring individuals tend, like a well-insulated building, to be able to withstand external pressures passively without expending much energy in doing so. Low-scoring individuals, on the other hand, have little insulation. External stresses reach them more easily, and, in order to maintain homeostasis, they must expend more energy. Constant exposure to external stresses and threatening situations can result in psychological exhaustion. (p. 7)

We would expect the person who succeeded despite the odds to score high on the Venturesome scale. Indeed, six of our participants demonstrated extreme scores on that scale. The other two characteristics on which our participants scored high are Abstract Thinking and Suspicious. Because academic success is correlated with Abstract Thinking, it is not unexpected that our participants would score high on this dimension. However, it is somewhat more difficult to account for why most of our participants scored high on the Suspicious scale.

What can we conclude from the information collected on the participants' personality? The personality measurements seem to suggest that individuals who succeed despite the odds, while

having their own unique combination of personality characteristics, share some common characteristics; these individuals
are sensitive, abstract thinking, venturesome, suspicious,
tense/driven, forthright, and self-sufficient. An interesting question is, Did these characteristics contribute to the participants'
succeeding despite the odds, or did they develop as a result of
the participants' life circumstances? Results of the current investigation are consistent with the mounting evidence (Garmezy, 1983; Werner and Smith, 1982) and theoretical orientation
(Cowen and Work, 1988; Richardson et al., 1990) suggesting that
there   may   be   a   personality   predisposition   in   resili-
ent/invulnerable children.

What significant factors, as indicated by extensive interviews,
appeared to be important in our participants succeeding despite
the odds? Some of these factors have already been described at
the end of each case study, that is, multigenerational family and
neighborhood influence, institutionalization, sporting activities,
and so on. However, while certain unique factors differentially
affected our participants, what factors seemed to be similar
across several participants? The quality of the participant's relationship with parents, particularly with mother, is one such
factor.

Among our participants who had intact families, strong, positive parental influence manifested itself either in a supportive
relationship, family structure with discipline, and/or religious
instruction. Even the participant who was placed in a foster
home reported receiving discipline and religious instruction.
Among the participants who were raised primarily in a single-
parent family, positive maternal influence manifested itself in a
supportive relationship or overprotectiveness. Regardless of
their parents' marital status, our participants, all of them re-
markably resilient, were raised in family environments characterized by either a supportive relationship with parent(s), strong
family structure with discipline, or considerable religious instruction.

Even though his mother died while he was very young, Chad
reports having her full support, love, and understanding; Kae's
parents were her "saving grace." Barbara made a similar observation relative to her foster parents. A quality of overprotec-

tiveness appeared to be significant in the lives of Waln, David, and, to a lesser degree, Chad. Family structure with discipline played a significant role in the upbringing of Barbara, Brenda, and Waln, while he was institutionalized. Chad, David, Warren, and Brenda were raised with significant religious influence.

Collectively, this information suggests that the quality of the parent/child relationship, including a sense of discipline and, to some degree, overprotectiveness and religious instruction appeared to be significant factors contributing to individuals succeeding despite the odds. These findings are not totally unexpected, given that other studies have pointed to the importance of these factors in the socialization process.

Encouraging student-teacher relationships also appeared to be significant in the lives of several participants. Both David and Barbara reported extensive encouragement from primary grade teachers, and Warren reported that a Job Corps teacher was a source of encouragement. Warren also reported being discouraged by a night school teacher, but the experience eventually proved motivating because it engendered in Warren the "I'll show him!" attitude. Brenda had a similar discouraging experience with a teacher and subsequently developed a similar attitude. In these latter cases, a negative teacher-student encounter proved motivating. Apparently, some motivating student-teacher encounters are vividly remembered nearly twenty-five years later. In addition, occupational and/or skills-building opportunities proved important in the developmental process of some of our participants. Clearly, Brenda and Warren benefited from the opportunities provided by governmental entitlement programs: Brenda received training assistance from Youth Corps and Warren from Job Corps. There are some indications that Chad may have been afforded job opportunities because of his status as an orphan.

Generally, our findings are consistent with other research (Garmezy, 1983) that used a very different population and methodology to identify three major factors as significant in helping children succeed despite the odds: personal predisposition; warm and supportive family environment; and external supports. The current investigation is most valuable in that it helped, albeit retrospectively, identify how these factors operated in the lives of specific individuals, thereby supporting the theoretical with specific case examples.

   In conclusion, all of our participants are now far removed from the childhood life circumstances that could have permanently debilitated them. The average person interacting with our participants would find it hard to believe that our participants experienced such difficulties when growing up. There remains no blatant hint of the past. To some extent, our participants are as different as night and day, yet they are similar in many respects. We have tried to highlight some of these similarities in the hope of shedding some light on factors that may be important in individuals overcoming the odds. Although our investigation has probably generated more questions than answers, it does lend support to a growing body of evidence that identifies specific, significant factors in the lives of those individuals who "succeed despite the odds."

References

Alan Guttmacher Institute. (1977). *11 million teenagers: What can be done about the epidemic of adolescent pregnancies in the United States?* New York: Alan Guttmacher Institute.

Brown S. (1985). Premarital sexual permissiveness among black adolescent females. *Social Psychology Quarterly*, 48 (4), 381–387.

Brown, W. (1983). *The Uroboros: Out of delinquency, a true story*. York, PA: William Gladden Foundation.

Cattell, R. B., Eber, H. W., & Tatsuoka, M. M. (1970). *Handbook for the Sixteen Personality Factor Questionnaire*. Champaign, IL: Institute for Personality and Ability Testing.

Cowen, E., & Work, W. (1988). Resilient children, psychological wellness, and primary prevention. *American Journal of Community Psychology*, 16 (4), 591–607.

Delaware Health Statistics. (May 1992). Department of Health and Social Services, Wilmington, DE.

Edelman, M. (1987). *Families in peril: An agenda for social change*. Harvard University Press: Cambridge, MA.

Feagans, L. (1983). A current view of learning disabilities. *Journal of Pediatrics*, 102 (4), 487–493.

Fein, E., Maluccio, A., Hamilton, V., & Ward, D. (1983). "After foster care: Outcomes of permanency planning for children." *Child Welfare*, 62 (6), 485–558.

Ferguson, J. (1990). Grads program in Ohio empowers parenting students to graduate. Paper presented at the Conference, Education and Training: The Route to Self-Sufficiency for Single Parents, Lexington, KY, June 10–12.

Fine, M. A., & Schwebel, A. I. (1991). Resiliency in Black children from single-parent families. In W. A. Rhodes and W. K. Brown (eds.), *Why some children succeed despite the odds.* New York: Praeger.

Fine, M. A., Schwebel, A. I., & Myers, L. J. (1987). Family stability in black families: Values underlying three different perspectives. *Journal of Comparative Family Studies, 18,* 1–23.

Garmezy, N. (1982). Stressors of Childhood. In N. Garmezy and M. Rutter (eds.), *Stress, coping, and development in children.* New York: McGraw-Hill.

Greene, J. (1987). Teenage Pregnancy and STDs. *The Female Patient, 12,* 46–61.

Harris, T., Brown, G., & Bifulco, A. (1990). Loss of parent in childhood and adult psychiatric disorder: A tentative overall model. *Development and Psychopathology, 2* (3), 311–328.

Hendrixson, L. (1983). Pregnant children: A socio-educational challenge. In *Annual Editions.* Guilford, Conn.: Dushkin Publishing Group.

Herbert, A. (1984) Teenage parents: Families without fathers. *The New Republic,* September, pp. 15–23.

Hernandez, D. (1988). Demographic trends and living arrangements of children. In E. M. Hetherington and J. D. Arasteh (eds.), *Impacts of divorce, single-parenting, and stepparenting on children.* Hillsdale, NJ: Erlbaum.

Hetherington, E. M., Stanley-Hagan, M., & Anderson, E. R. (1989). Marital transitions: A child's perspective. *American Psychologist, 44* (2), 303–312.

Hulbert, A. (1984). Children as parents. *The New Republic,* September, pp. 15–23.

Krug, S. E. (1981). *Interpreting 16PF Profile Patterns.* Champaign, IL: Institute for Personality and Ability Testing.

Lerner, J. (1988). *Learning disabilities.* Princeton, NJ: Houghton Mifflin.

Maluccio, A., Fein, E., Hamilton, V., Klier, J., & Ward, D. (1980). Beyond permanency planning. *Child Welfare, 59,* 515–530.

McHolland, J. (1976). *Human Potential Seminar: A positive approach to self-development.* Evanston, IL: National Center for Human Potential.

Merki, M. B., & Merki, D. (1993). *Health: A guide to wellness.* Columbus, OH: Macmillan/McGraw-Hill.

Moynihan, D. P. (1965). *The Negro family: The case for national action.* Washington, DC: Office of Policy Planning and Research, U.S. Department of Labor.

Murphy, Lois. (1962). *Paths toward mastery*. New York: Basic Books.

Myers, P. I., & Hammill, D. D. (1990). *Learning disability*. Austin, Tex.: Pro-Ed.

Nye, I. (1977). *School-age parenthood: Consequence for babies, mothers, fathers, grandmothers, and others*. Pullman, Wash.: Washington State University.

Papalia, D., & Olds, S. (1992). *Human development*. New York: McGraw-Hill.

Papalia, D., & Olds, S. (1989). *Human development*. New York: McGraw-Hill.

Papalia, D., & Olds, S. (1986). *Human development*. New York: McGraw-Hill.

Ragan, P., & McGlashan, T. (1987). Childhood parental death and adult psychology. *American Journal of Psychiatry, 143* (2), 153–157.

Rhodes, W. A., & Brown, W. K. (eds.). (1991). *Why some children succeed despite the odds*. New York: Praeger.

Rhodes, W., Duncan, J., & Hall, O. (1987). Peer counseling in juvenile awareness: A demonstration project. *The Clearing House, 60* (6), 273–275.

Rhodes, W., & Stevenson, H. (1991). Risk and resilience in teenagers who avoid pregnancy. In W. Rhodes and W. Brown (eds.), *Why some children succeed despite the odds*. New York: Praeger.

Richardson, G., Neiger, B., Jensen, S., & Kumpfer, K. (1990). The resiliency model. *Health Education, 21* (6), 33–39.

Sutherland, E. (1947). *Principles of criminology*. Philadelphia: J. B. Lippincott.

Tennant, C. (1988). Parental loss in childhood. *Archives of General Psychiatry, 45*, 1045–1050.

Thyer, B., Himle, J., & Fischer, D. (1988). Is parental death a selective precursor to either panic disorder or agoraphobia? A test of the separation anxiety hypothesis. *Journal of Anxiety Disorders, 2* (4), 33–338.

Walters, J. (1975). Birth defects and adolescent pregnancies, *Journal of Home Economics, 67* (6), 23–33.

Walters, L., Walters, J., & McKenry, P. (1987). Differentiation of girls at risk of early pregnancy from the general population of adolescents. *Journal of Genetic Psychology, 148*, 19–29.

Werner, E. E., & Smith, B. A. (1982). *Vulnerable but invincible: A longitudinal study of resilient children and youth*. New York: McGraw-Hill.

Widom, C. (1991). The role of placement experiences in mediating the criminal consequences of early childhood victimization. *American Journal of Orthopsychiatry, 61*, (2), 195–209.

Wilder, Douglas. (1991). Straight talk on black families. *Readers Digest*,
    July.
Zahner, G., & Murphy, J. (1989). Loss in childhood: Anxiety in adult-
    hood. *Comprehensive Psychiatry, 30* (6), 553–563.

Index

About the Authors

WARREN A. RHODES is Professor of Psychology, Delaware
State University. He is the co-editor of *Why Some Children Succeed
Despite the Odds* (Praeger, 1991).

KIM HOEY is a freelance writer.